Sandra Lee

semi-homemade®

Comfort Food

This book belongs to:

____

Chicken Fried Steak with Southern Gravy, *page 190*

Solution-based
Enterprise that
Motivates,
Inspires, and
Helps
Organize and
Manage time, while
Enriching
Modern life by
Adding
Dependable shortcuts
Every day.

This book is printed on acid-free paper.

Published by John Wiley & Sons, Inc., Hoboken, New Jersey, in partnership with SL Books.

Published simultaneously in Canada.

Cover photo and selected author photos by Ed Ouellette.

For general information on our other products and services or for technical support, please contact our Customer Care Department within the United States at (800) 762-2974, outside the United States at (317) 572-3993 or fax (317) 572-4002.

Wiley also publishes its books in a variety of electronic formats. Some content that appears in print may not be available in electronic books. For more information about Wiley products, visit our web site at www.wiley.com.

Library of Congress Cataloging-in-Publication Data:
Lee, Sandra, 1966-
Semi-homemade comfort food/Sandra Lee.
p. cm.
Includes index.
ISBN 978-0-470-64594-9 (pbk.)
1. Quick and easy cooking. 2. Comfort food. 3. Low budget cooking 4. Cooking--United States 5. Grocery shopping 6. Cookbooks. I. Title.
TX833.5.L4156 2010
641.5'55--dc22
2010033574

Printed in the United States of America.

10 9 8 7 6 5 4 3 2 1

John Wiley & Sons, Inc.

get our Magazine

You'll find everything you need to simplify your busy life—from money saving tips to dazzling tablescape projects and more quick-and-easy recipes.

QUICK, HEALTHY MEALS

Enjoy recipes for hearty but healthy meals that your family will enjoy. You'll also find tips to lighten up other recipes and menus.

seasonal parties

Every issue includes affordable and attainable party ideas complete with menus, recipes, and tablescape ideas to suit any budget.

family favorites

Practical but impressive recipes, such as succulent roast chicken and vegetables, are great for both weeknights and special occasions.

Cocktail Time

Indulge in refreshing cocktails paired with amazing appetizers for simply fabulous fare with friends.

Table of Contents

Simple Servings of Something Special

"Comfort food says love—and that's what makes the world go round." — Sandra Lee

Comfort food is love on a plate—and a little bit of comfort goes a long way towards making life better. Your favorite comfort food may be a steamy bowl of chili eaten while you're cuddled up in a snuggly blanket enjoying a movie. It may be a turkey with stuffing or a tender pot roast dinner with mashed potatoes all smothered in thick brown gravy. Or it may be a crunchy and gooey grilled cheese and bacon sandwich paired with a bowl of creamy tomato soup. It's all feel-good food—and sometimes it hits the spot like nothing else will.

When I am exceptionally excited about what I am about to eat, particularly if it's something sweet like a snickerdoodle cookie or a decadent caramel pecan bar, I close my eyes as I take that first bite so that all my senses are focused on the taste and texture that fills my mouth. Close your own eyes and envision your favorite comfort food, then flip through these pages and find the best recipe to create your food fantasy. Stick to the ones that will fill your soul as much as your tummy.

All of these recipes were created for your comfort and happiness. Every day of every season is the perfect day for comfort food because comfort food says love—and that's what makes the world go round.

Cheers to a happy, healthy home,

Sandra Lee

Molasses Snickerdoodles, *page 12*

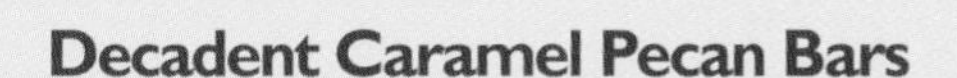

Decadent Caramel Pecan Bars

Nonstick butter-flavor cooking spray
24 pecan shortbread cookies
2 sticks (1 cup) butter
1 1/4 cups packed dark brown sugar
1/3 cup light-color corn syrup
2 tablespoons whipping cream
2 cups pecans, chopped
1 teaspoon vanilla

1. Preheat oven to 350°F. Spray a 9-inch square baking pan with cooking spray. Place shortbread cookies in a food processor; cover and pulse until in fine crumbs. Cut 1/2 cup of the butter into small pieces. Add butter pieces to crumbs in food processor. Cover and pulse until mixture comes together. Press crumb mixture into bottom of the prepared pan. Bake in preheated oven for 15 minutes. Cool in pan on a wire rack.
2. In a medium saucepan, combine the remaining 1/2 cup butter, the brown sugar, corn syrup, and whipping cream; cook and stir over medium-high heat just until boiling. Boil for 1 minute; remove from heat. Stir in pecans and vanilla. Pour pecan mixture over cooled shortbread crust. Bake in preheated oven about 20 minutes or until bubbling. Cool in pan on a wire rack. Cut into bars.

Comforting Cocktails At the end of a hectic day, it's a treat to sip something while dinner cooks—or to indulge in after dinner as dessert. Whether it's a cooldown or a warm-up, it always helps to unwind.

Cold Cocktails

Gin Plush: In a large cocktail glass, combine 4 ice cubes, 1/3 cup gin, 1/4 cup guava nectar, 1/4 cup pineapple juice, 1/4 cup orange juice, and 1/4 cup chilled club soda. Stir; serve immediately. Makes 1 serving.

Sour Apple Martini: In a cocktail shaker, combine 4 ice cubes, 3 tablespoons apple sourball mix, 3 tablespoons vodka, and 2 teaspoons sweet vermouth. Cover and shake for 15 seconds. Strain into a martini glass and garnish with an apple slice. Makes 1 serving.

Champagne Punch: In a large punch bowl or pitcher, stir together 1 (20-ounce) can crushed pineapple in heavy syrup, 1 cup fresh lemon juice, 1 cup maraschino cherry juice, 1 cup dark rum, and 1/2 cup brandy. Refrigerate 30 minutes. Right before serving, add 1 (750-ml) bottle chilled champagne. Makes 6 servings.

Cubana Rum: In a cocktail shaker, combine 1/3 cup apricot nectar, 1/4 cup fresh lime juice, 1/4 cup apricot brandy, 1/4 cup light rum, and 4 ice cubes. Cover and shake for 15 seconds. Strain into a glass. Makes 1 serving.

Hot Cocktails

Cafe à la Orange: In a 4-quart slow cooker, stir together 6 cups water, ⅔ cup sugar, ½ cup chocolate liqueur, ½ cup orange liqueur, 6 tablespoons instant coffee crystals, 2 tablespoons unsweetened cocoa powder. Cover and heat on low for 2 to 3 hours. Stir in 2 cups half-and-half. Turn cooker to warm setting . Stir 1 teaspoon orange extract into 1 (8-ounce) container whipped topping. Serve coffee topped with whipped topping. Sprinkle with cocoa powder and orange peel curls. Makes 8 servings.

Peach and Apricot Cider: In a 4-quart slow cooker, combine 2 cans (11.5 ounces each) peach nectar, 2 cans (11.5 ounces each) apricot nectar, 1 bag (12-ounce) frozen peach slices, 3 cups water, 1 cup brown sugar, 1 cup bourbon, ½ cup lemon juice, 1 teaspoon ground allspice, and 2 cinnamon sticks. Cover; heat on low for 2 hours. Discard cinnamon sticks. Turn cooker to warm. Serve with additional cinnamon sticks. Makes 12 servings.

Hot Mulled Pineapple Juice: Make a spice bag with 2 cinnamon sticks, broken; ¼ teaspoon whole cloves; and 1 tablespoon grated orange peel. In a saucepan, combine 5 cups pineapple juice and spice bag. Simmer on medium-low heat for 20 minutes. Stir in 1 ounce spiced rum per serving (optional). Garnish with cinnamon stick and pineapple wedge. Makes 4 servings.

Mexican Coffee: Brew 4 cups of coffee, adding 1 tablespoon unsweetened cocoa powder and ½ teaspoon ground cinnamon to the ground coffee beans in the filter. Sweeten to taste with sugar. Top each serving with whipped cream and a sprinkle of cinnamon. Add 1 ounce orange liqueur and 1 ounce tequila to each mug before serving (optional). Makes 4 servings.

Triple-Thick Hot Chocolate: In a bowl, mix 9 tablespoons hot cocoa mix and 4 tablespoons cornstarch. Add ½ cup low-fat milk, 2 teaspoons vanilla, and 2 tablespoons softened butter. Stir to make a paste. In a saucepan, bring 4 cups of low-fat milk to boil. Whisk in paste, stirring until thickened. Pour into 4 mugs. Stir 1 ounce *Baileys Irish Cream* into each mug (optional). Top with whipped cream. Makes 4 servings.

Sandra's Secret Comfort Food

Nice Nibbles

Chicken Soup with Wonton Dumplings and Creamy Tuna Sandwich: In a large saucepan, combine 2 quarts chicken broth, 1 teaspoon brown sugar, fresh ginger to taste, red pepper flakes to taste, 1 tablespoon lime juice, 1 tablespoon minced garlic, and 3 tablespoons soy sauce. Bring to a boil over high heat. Boil for 5 minutes. Add some snow peas, sliced shiitake mushrooms, chopped cilantro to taste, and 1 bag (13-ounce) mini cheese ravioli. Bring to boil again; reduce heat to medium and simmer for 5 minutes. Serve with tuna salad sandwiches layered with sliced tomato and butterhead lettuce. Makes 6 servings.

Crispy Bacon Grilled Cheese and Tomato Soup: Lay a slice of cheddar or American cheese on a piece of bread. Cut 2 pieces of cooked bacon in half and place on cheese. Top with another slice of the same cheese—or with a slice of pepper jack. Spread butter on outside of sandwich. Toast in a skillet until golden brown, turning once. Serve with tomato soup topped with croutons and herbed sour cream. Makes 1 serving.

Sour Cream Hash Brown Casserole: I like to serve this as a dip. Spray a 9×13-inch baking dish with cooking spray. Pour 1 bag (30-ounce) hash browns into pan. Toss with 1½ cups shredded cheddar cheese. In a bowl, combine 1 (14-ounce) can cream of celery soup, 4 tablespoons melted butter, 2 cups sour cream, and 1 chopped onion. Pour over hash browns. Top with 1 cup shredded cheddar. Sprinkle 1 tablespoon taco seasoning over cheese. Bake at 350°F for 40 minutes, or until bubbly. Makes 8 servings (as a casserole).

Main Meals

Grandma Dicie's Buttermilk Fried Chicken with Mashed Potatoes and Milk Gravy: In a large bowl, combine 1 tablespoon dried Italian seasoning, salt and pepper, 1 sliced onion, and 1 quart buttermilk. Marinate 1 chicken, cut up, with buttermilk mixture in a large resealable plastic bag in refrigerator for 8 hours. In a large shallow bowl, stir together 4 cups flour with 1 tablespoon *Old Bay Seasoning®* and salt and pepper. In a large heavy skillet, heat ½-inch vegetable oil over medium heat. As oil is heating, remove a piece of chicken from marinade, shaking to remove drips. Dip in flour and set on a platter. Repeat with remaining chicken. When oil is hot, fry chicken in skillet, uncovered, for 15 minutes, turning to brown evenly. Reduce heat; cover pan and cook another 5 to 10 minutes until chicken is cooked. Place chicken on rack placed on a baking sheet in a warm oven. Serve with hot mashed potatoes and *McCormick® Country Gravy Mix* prepared according to package directions, substituting half the water for milk. Season with lots of black pepper to taste. Makes 4 to 6 servings.

Twice-Baked Lasagna: Thaw 1 package (38-ounce) of *Stouffer's® Lasagna Italiano* in refrigerator. Remove top layer; set aside. Sprinkle 1½ cups shredded Italian cheese blend and 2 links crumbled cooked Italian sausage over top. Replace top layer. Bake at 350°F for 25 minutes. Makes 6 servings.

Quick Comforts: When your kitchen is stocked with staples such as ham, turkey breast, frozen mashed potatoes, seasoning mixes, and casserole mixes, a simple, satisfying meal is just minutes away.

Baked Brilliance

Warm Chocolate Coffee Brownie: Prepare a brownie mix, adding 1 teaspoon vanilla, 2 tablespoons instant espresso powder, and substituting leftover brewed coffee for the liquid. For an adult version, drizzle the warm brownies with a couple tablespoons of *Kahlúa®* right before serving. Cut into 12 squares. Top with coffee ice cream. Makes 12 servings.

Molasses Snickerdoodles: In a large bowl, stir together 1 (17.5-ounce) pouch sugar cookie mix, ½ cup flour, ¼ cup packed brown sugar, 2 teaspoons pumpkin pie spice, 1½ teaspoons ground ginger, ¼ teaspoon ground cloves, and ¼ teaspoon ground black pepper. Add ½ cup melted butter, 1 egg, and 2 tablespoons molasses. Stir until a stiff dough forms. Combine ¼ cup sugar and 1 tablespoon cinnamon. Roll a heaping tablespoon of dough into a ball. Roll ball in sugar mixture. Place 2 inches apart on cookie sheets. Flatten cookies with bottom of a glass. Bake 14 to 16 minutes at 375°F until edges are golden brown. Cool on cookie sheets for 5 minutes.

Gingerbread Pancakes: In a bowl, combine 1½ cups gingerbread cake mix, ½ cup flour, 2 eggs, 2 teaspoons vanilla, and 1 cup water. Let rest 30 minutes. Heat a skillet over medium heat and add a bit of butter. When butter has melted, pour ¼ cup batter in pan for each pancake. When pancakes are covered with bubbles, flip and cook an additional 30 seconds. Top with butter pecan ice cream and maple syrup. Makes 18 (3-inch) pancakes.

Hot Strawberry Pop-Tarts® Sundaes: Toast 4 strawberry *Pop-Tarts*. While tarts are toasting, stir 1 teaspoon vanilla into 2 cups thawed sweetened sliced strawberries. Break the hot pastries in pieces. Line two sundae dishes or bowls with the pieces. Top with vanilla ice cream, strawberries, and whipped topping.

Sweet Comforts There's some truth to the cliché that a pint of ice cream cures a broken heart (well, maybe not cures, but certainly makes the brokenhearted feel better). Something sweet always brings a smile to your face.

Incredible Ice Cream

100 Grand® Ice Cream Whip: Using a sharp knife, cut 2 (1.5-ounce) *100 Grand®* candy bars into pieces. Place in a small plastic bag and freeze for at least 2 hours. In a blender container, combine frozen candy bar pieces, 24 ounces vanilla ice cream, and ½ cup cold milk. Blend on high for about 30 seconds or until well mixed. Pour into two 12-ounce glasses. Drizzle with chocolate syrup. Makes 2 servings.

Snacks & Starters

The "small plates" you eat to whet your appetite for the rest of the meal can be the most comforting ones of all because they come to the rescue when you are the hungriest. These tasty bites include stuffed mushrooms, cheesy fondue, and yummy savory pastries (everyone loves those!). Serve them between meals as a snack, at the beginning of a meal as a starter—or simply when you're craving a delicious nibble.

New
McCormick
Cinnamon Sugar Grinder
Grill Mates
Montreal Chicken
Grinder
Seasoning
Cinnamon Grinder
Gourmet Collection
Toasted Sesame Seed
NET WT 1.62 OZ (45g)
Ground Black Pepper
with Panko Bread

Pepper Steak on a Stick

Prep 20 minutes **Marinate** 2 to 3 hours **Grill** 4 minutes **Makes** 4 servings

BEEF AND MARINADE

- 1 ¼ **pounds boneless beef sirloin steak**
- 1 **teaspoon seasoned pepper blend, *McCormick®***
- 1 **teaspoon garlic salt, *McCormick®***
- ½ **cup extra virgin olive oil**
- ½ **cup frozen orange juice concentrate, thawed, *Minute Maid®***
- ½ **cup pineapple juice, *Dole®***
- 1 **tablespoon low-sodium soy sauce, *Kikkoman®***
- 1 **teaspoon stone-ground mustard, *Inglehoffer®***

ORANGE CHILI SAUCE

- ½ **cup chili sauce, *Heinz®***
- ½ **cup orange marmalade, *Smucker's®***
- 2 **teaspoons Worcestershire sauce, *Lea & Perrins®***

1. Season beef with pepper blend and garlic salt. Slice beef across the grain into ¼-inch-thick slices; set aside.

2. For marinade, in a large zip-top plastic bag, combine olive oil, orange juice concentrate, pineapple juice, soy sauce, and mustard. Add beef strips to bag. Squeeze out air and seal. Shake bag to distribute marinade. Marinate in the refrigerator for 2 to 3 hours.

3. For the orange chili sauce, in a small saucepan, stir together chili sauce, marmalade, and Worcestershire sauce until well mixed. Simmer over medium heat until marmalade dissolves. Set aside.

4. Set up grill for direct cooking over high heat. Remove beef strips from marinade and discard marinade. Thread beef on wooden skewers, accordion style. Place skewers on hot grill. Cook for 2 to 3 minutes per side. Serve beef sticks warm with orange chili sauce on the side.

Honey Pigs

Start to Finish 30 minutes **Makes** 16 servings

- 1 **pound ground pork sausage, *Jimmy Dean®***
- 1 **tablespoon chopped fresh thyme**
- 1 **teaspoon bottled crushed garlic, *Gourmet Garden®***
- 1 **teaspoon salt**
- ¼ **teaspoon ground black pepper**
- 1 **packet (about ¾ cup) pork coating, *Shake 'N Bake®***
- **Extra virgin olive oil for frying**
- **Orange blossom honey (optional)**
- **Fresh thyme sprigs (optional)**

1. In a medium bowl, combine sausage, 1 tablespoon chopped thyme, garlic, salt, and pepper until well mixed. Shape into sixteen 1½-inch balls. Press balls into 2-inch round patties.

2. Pour coating mixture into a pie plate. Dredge each pork patty in coating.

3. In a large skillet, heat ¼ inch of oil over medium-high heat. Working in batches, place patties in pan with a spatula and fry for 3 to 5 minutes per side. Remove and drain on paper towels. (Add more oil to pan between batches, if necessary.)

4. Drizzle honey (optional) over each patty and garnish with thyme (optional). Serve immediately.

Hash Brown Cake and Sausages

Prep 30 minutes **Bake** 20 minutes **Makes** 6 servings

- 1 bag (20-ounce) refrigerated hash browns, *Simply Potatoes®*
- 2 teaspoons lemon herb seasoning, *McCormick®*
- 1 teaspoon salt
- ¼ teaspoon ground black pepper
- 2 tablespoons butter, melted
- 1 tablespoon extra virgin olive oil
- ⅓ cup shredded 3-cheese blend, *DiGiorno®*
- 2 bottles (12 ounces each) pale ale
- 4 links fresh bratwurst, *Johnsonville®*
- Chopped fresh chives (optional)
- Sour cream (optional)

1. Preheat oven to 450°F.

2. In a large bowl, toss hash browns with lemon herb seasoning, salt, and pepper. In a small bowl, stir together melted butter and olive oil; pour half the mixture over hash browns and toss together.

3. In a large cast-iron skillet, heat the remaining butter-oil mixture over medium-high heat. Arrange one-third of the hash browns on the bottom of skillet. Sprinkle cheese into remaining hash browns in bowl and toss together. Spread over first layer of hash browns and press with a spatula. Cook for 4 minutes, pressing with spatula. Transfer skillet to the oven. Bake for 20 to 25 minutes, pressing with spatula halfway through cooking time.

4. Meanwhile, in a large saucepan, bring ale to a simmer and add bratwurst. Simmer for 25 to 30 minutes or until cooked through.

5. Remove hash browns from oven and invert skillet over a cutting board to remove potatoes. Cut hash brown cake into wedges; top with sausage slices. Serve with fresh chives and sour cream (optional).

Pigs in a Cheese Blanket

Prep 20 minutes **Bake** 12 minutes **Makes** 48 servings

PIGS

Nonstick cooking spray, *Pam*®

- 2 **cans (8 ounces each) refrigerated crescent dinner rolls, *Pillsbury*®**
- 10 **slices sharp cheddar cheese slices, *Tillamook*®**
- 1 **package (14-ounce) Li'l beef smokies, *Hillshire Farm*®**

DIPPING SAUCE

- ½ **cup Dijon mustard, *Ingelhoffer*®**
- ¼ **cup mayonnaise, *Best Foods*®/ *Hellmann's*®**
- 2 **tablespoons honey, *Sue Bee*®**

1. Preheat oven to 375°F. Lightly spray two baking sheets with cooking spray; set aside.

2. For the pigs, unroll both cans of the dough and separate into 16 triangles total. Cut each triangle into three smaller triangles. Cut each slice of cheese into five pieces about ½ inch wide.

3. Place a piece of cheese on each triangle, then a sausage on the widest side of each triangle. Fold narrow point of dough over each sausage. Place, point side down, on prepared baking sheets.*

4. Bake for 12 to 15 minutes or until golden, rotating the baking sheets halfway through baking. Remove immediately from baking sheets.

5. For the dipping sauce, in a medium bowl, stir together mustard, mayonnaise, and honey. Serve pigs warm with dipping sauce.

***Note:** If desired, before baking brush each roll lightly with ketchup and sprinkle with poppy seeds. Or brush lightly with Dijon mustard and sprinkle with sesame seeds.

Bruschetta with Herb and Almond Tapenade

Start to Finish 10 minutes **Makes** 2½ cups

- 1½ **cups mixed fresh herbs, such as oregano, chives, thyme, tarragon, dill, basil, or parsley, finely chopped**
- ¾ **cup slivered almonds, toasted and finely chopped, *Diamond®***
- 1½ **cups prepared olive tapenade, *DeLallo®***
- 1 **tablespoon diced jalapeño, *Ortega®***
- 1 **tablespoon frozen lemon juice, thawed, *Minute Maid®***
- **Toasted baguette slices**

1. In a medium bowl, stir together herbs, almonds, tapenade, jalapeño, and lemon juice until well mixed.

2. Serve with toasted baguette slices.

Cheese and Ale Fondue

Start to Finish 15 minutes **Makes** 12 servings

- ¼ **cup butter**
- ¼ **cup all-purpose flour**
- 1 **bottle (12-ounce) lager-style beer, *Samuel Adams Boston Lager®***
- ½ **teaspoon dry mustard, *McCormick®***
- ½ **teaspoon Worcestershire sauce, *Lea & Perrins®***
- ¼ **teaspoon cayenne pepper, *McCormick®***
- 4 **cups shredded cheddar cheese, *Sargento®***
- **Crusty bread cubes, soft pretzels, or assorted fresh vegetables, such as carrots, broccoli, and cauliflower**

1. In a medium saucepan, melt butter over medium heat. Stir in flour; cook for 1 to 2 minutes, stirring constantly. Add beer. Slowly bring to a boil. Reduce heat and cook until mixture thickens to the consistency of heavy cream, stirring occasionally.

2. Stir in mustard, Worcestershire sauce, and cayenne pepper; gradually add cheese, stirring over low heat until cheese is melted.

3. Serve warm with crusty bread cubes, soft pretzels, or vegetables.

Turkish Rolls

Prep 20 minutes **Bake** 25 minutes **Makes** 24 appetizers

Nonstick olive oil cooking spray, *Mazola®*

½ **cup garlic stuffed green olives, chopped, *Mezzetta®***

½ **cup pitted kalamata olives, chopped, *Peloponnese®***

⅓ **cup crumbled feta cheese with lemon, garlic, and oregano, *Athenos®***

3 **tablespoons sliced almonds, *Planters®***

3 **tablespoons golden raisins, *Sun-Maid®***

½ **teaspoon chai spice blend, *McCormick®***

8 **sheets frozen phyllo dough, thawed, *Athens®***

1. Preheat oven to 350°F. Spray 2 baking sheets with cooking spray; set aside.

2. In a medium bowl, combine olives, feta cheese, almonds, raisins, and chai spice; set aside.

3. Lay one sheet of phyllo dough on a flat surface. (Keep remaining phyllo covered with a clean dish towel as you work.) Spray an even layer of cooking spray over entire sheet and top with another phyllo sheet. Continue to make four layers. With a sharp knife, cut dough to make 12 rectangular pieces.

4. Spread a heaping teaspoon of olive mixture along the shorter side of one of the phyllo pieces, leaving ½ inch on each side. Tightly roll short end toward other end to form a cylinder. Spray end with cooking spray, secure seam, and place on prepared baking sheet, seam side down. Repeat entire procedure to make a total of 24 pieces.

5. Bake for 25 to 30 minutes or until rolls are golden brown. Cool for 5 minutes before serving.

Pesto-Stuffed Mushrooms

Prep 20 minutes **Bake** 20 minutes **Makes** 24 mushrooms

- **Nonstick cooking spray, *Pam*®**
- **24 large fresh mushrooms**
- **4 tablespoons extra virgin olive oil**
- **1 cup sourdough stuffing mix, *Stove Top*®**
- **½ cup boiling water**
- **1 cup ricotta cheese, *Precious*®**
- **¾ cup shredded mozzarella cheese, *Sargento*®**
- **¼ cup grated Parmesan cheese, *Sargento*®**
- **2 tablespoons pesto, *Classico*®**
- **2 teaspoons bottled garlic blend, *Gourmet Garden*®**

1. Preheat oven to 375°F. Spray a rimmed baking sheet with nonstick cooking spray; set aside.

2. Wipe mushrooms clean with paper towels. Remove stems and discard; if necessary, hollow out the caps. Using a pastry brush, coat inside and outside of mushrooms with olive oil.

3. In a medium bowl, combine stuffing mix and boiling water. Cover bowl; let stand for 5 minutes or until stuffing mix is slightly softened. Stir in ricotta cheese, mozzarella, 2 tablespoons of the Parmesan cheese, pesto, and garlic blend. Fill each mushroom with stuffing mixture. Arrange mushrooms on prepared baking sheet; sprinkle with remaining Parmesan cheese.

4. Bake for 20 to 25 minutes or until golden. Serve immediately.

Crispy Onion-Crusted Portobellos

Start to Finish 25 minutes **Makes** 10 servings

- **Vegetable oil for frying, *Wesson*®**
- **1 cup french-fried onions, *French's*®**
- **½ cup bread crumbs, *Progresso*®**
- **Salt and ground black pepper**
- **½ cup egg substitute, *Egg Beaters*®**
- **1 package (8-ounce) sliced portobello mushrooms, *Monterey*®**
- **Desired purchased dip**

1. In a medium saucepan, heat 1 inch of oil to 350°F.

2. Place french-fried onions in a large zip-top bag. Press out air and seal. Use a rolling pin to crush onions in bag. Pour crushed onions into a pie plate and mix with bread crumbs. Season to taste with salt and pepper.

3. Pour egg substitute into a shallow bowl. Dip a portobello slice in egg substitute and shake off excess. Dredge in bread crumb mixture until well coated; place on a rack. Repeat with remaining portobellos.

4. Working in batches, fry portobellos about 2 minutes per side or until golden brown. Remove with tongs and drain on paper towels. Serve immediately with desired dip.

Fruited Cheese Puffs

Prep 25 minutes **Bake** 25 minutes **Cool** 5 minutes **Makes** 16 servings

- **1 sheet puff pastry, thawed, *Pepperidge Farm*®**
- **1 egg**
- **1 teaspoon water**
- **3 tablespoons goat cheese**
- **2 tablespoons + 1 teaspoon cream cheese, softened, *Philadelphia*®**
- **⅔ cup dried mixed fruit, finely chopped, *Sun-Maid*®**

1. Preheat oven to 400°F. Line two baking sheets with parchment paper; set aside.

2. On a lightly floured surface, unroll puff pastry sheet. Using a rolling pin, roll pastry to a 14×10-inch rectangle. Cut pastry into sixteen 3½×2½-inch rectangles.

3. Stir together egg and water; set aside. In a medium bowl, stir together goat cheese and softened cream cheese until well mixed. Spread 1 teaspoon of cheese mixture in middle of a pastry rectangle; top with 2 teaspoons of the chopped dried fruit. Using a pastry brush, brush egg wash on edges of pastry. Bring corners of the pastry together and pinch seams together with a fork. Repeat with remaining pastry, cheese, and dried fruit to make 16 puffs total.

4. Arrange puffs on baking sheets. Refrigerate for 15 minutes. Remove from refrigerator and brush tops with remaining egg wash.

5. Bake for 25 to 30 minutes or until puffed and golden. Remove from oven and cool for 5 minutes. Serve warm.

Greek Cups

Prep 30 minutes **Bake** 16 minutes **Makes** 30 appetizers

- **Nonstick butter-flavor cooking spray, *Mazola*®**
- 15 **sheets frozen phyllo dough, thawed, *Athens*®**
- 1 **box (10-ounce) frozen chopped spinach, thawed and well drained, *Birds Eye*®**
- 1 **container (4-ounce) crumbled feta cheese, *Athenos*®**
- ¼ **cup pitted kalamata olives, chopped, *Peloponnese*®**
- 1 **egg**
- ¼ **cup plain yogurt, *Dannon*®**
- 1 **tablespoon Greek seasoning, *McCormick*®**
- 2 **teaspoons frozen lemon juice, thawed, *Minute Maid*®**

1. Preheat oven to 350°F. Spray 30 muffin cups with cooking spray; set aside.

2. Unroll phyllo dough. Lay one sheet of phyllo dough on a flat surface. (Keep remaining phyllo covered with a clean dish towel as you work.) Spray an even layer of cooking spray over entire sheet and top with another phyllo sheet. Continue with four more phyllo sheets to make a six-layer stack. With a sharp knife, cut phyllo stack into 12 squares. Press each phyllo square into a muffin cup. Repeat with another six sheets of the phyllo. Halve the remaining three phyllo sheets crosswise. Use halved sheets to make another phyllo stack; cut this stack into six squares and press each into a muffin cup.

3. Bake for 8 to 10 minutes. Remove and set aside.

4. In a large bowl, combine spinach, feta cheese, olives, egg, yogurt, Greek seasoning, and lemon juice until well mixed. Spoon about 1 tablespoon spinach mixture into each phyllo cup. Bake for 8 to 10 minutes more or until heated through. Serve immediately.

Soup & Sandwich Combos

The most classic soup and sandwich combination may be grilled cheese and tomato soup, but if you want to branch out a bit, try Potato-Tomato Bisque with Bacon and Blue on Rye—or maybe Creamy Cauliflower Soup with Mini Pepperoni Calzones. Perfect for lunch or a light supper, a hearty sandwich paired with something warm to sip from a spoon soothes and satisfies.

McCormick
McCormick
SEASONING MIX

HOURS

Sweet Potato and Ginger Soup

Start to Finish 25 minutes **Makes** 8 servings

- 1 bag (24-ounce) frozen cut sweet potatoes, *Ore-Ida® Steam n' Mash®*
- 2 tablespoons extra virgin olive oil
- 1 medium leek, white part only, cleaned and thinly sliced
- 1½ cups shredded carrots, *Ready Pac®*
- 4 cups less-sodium chicken broth, *Swanson®*
- 1 tablespoon + 1 teaspoon bottled minced ginger, *Gourmet Garden®*
- Salt and ground black pepper
- ½ cup fat-free plain yogurt
- Chopped fresh cilantro (optional)

1. Microwave sweet potatoes according to package directions; set aside.

2. In a soup pot, heat oil over medium-high heat. Add leek and carrots; cook and stir for 4 to 5 minutes or until they begin to soften. Stir in sweet potatoes, broth, and the 1 tablespoon minced ginger. Bring to a boil; reduce heat to low. Simmer for 15 minutes.

3. Transfer mixture to a blender (work in batches if necessary). Cover and blend until smooth. Return soup to pot and reheat. Season to taste with salt and pepper. Stir in the remaining 1 teaspoon minced ginger. Ladle soup into serving bowls. Top each serving with yogurt and chopped cilantro (optional).

Grilled Chèvre and Sweet Onion Sandwich

Start to Finish 20 minutes **Makes** 8 servings

- 16 slices Swiss cheese, *Sargento®*
- 16 slices dark rye bread, *Oroweat®*
- 1½ cups sweet onion jam, *Stonewall Kitchen®*
- 2 logs (5.5 ounces each) goat cheese, sliced ¼-inch thick, *Silver Goat®*
- 1 stick (½ cup) butter, softened

1. Make sandwiches by laying 2 of the Swiss cheese slices on a piece of rye bread. Top with 3 tablespoons of the onion jam, 3 slices of the goat cheese, and another slice of the rye bread. Repeat with remaining ingredients.

2. Heat a large heavy-bottom skillet or griddle over medium-low heat. Spread butter on one side of a sandwich and place in skillet. Spread butter on other side of sandwich. Grill sandwiches about 6 minutes or until Swiss is melted and bread is toasted, turning once.

3. Serve immediately or keep sandwiches warm and toasty in a 200°F oven until ready to serve.

Potato-Tomato Bisque

Start to Finish 30 minutes **Makes** 4 servings

- **2 tablespoons butter**
- **2 large leeks, white part only, well washed and chopped**
- **4 cloves roasted garlic, *Christopher Ranch*®**
- **4 cups reduced-sodium chicken broth, *Swanson*®**
- **1 bag (24-ounce) frozen garlic-seasoned potatoes, *Ore-Ida*® *Steam n' Mash*®**
- **1 can (14.5-ounce) petite diced tomatoes, *Hunt's*®**
- **½ cup light cream or milk**
- **Salt and ground black pepper**
- **Finely chopped fresh chives (optional)**

1. In a large saucepan, melt butter over medium-high heat. Add leeks and garlic; cook and stir about 5 minutes or until tender. Add chicken broth, frozen potatoes, and tomatoes. Bring to a boil; reduce heat. Simmer for 15 minutes. Remove from heat and cool.

2. Transfer mixture to a blender (work in batches if necessary). Cover and puree until smooth. (Soup can be stored in refrigerator for up to two days at this point.) Stir in cream and season to taste with salt and pepper. Top with chopped chives (optional).

Bacon and Blue on Rye

Start to Finish 10 minutes **Makes** 4 servings

- **16 slices fully cooked bacon, *Tyson*®**
- **8 slices light rye bread, *Oroweat*®**
- **⅓ cup creamy blue cheese dressing, *Bob's Big Boy*®**
- **4 tablespoons crumbled blue cheese, *Sargento*®**
- **2 roma tomatoes, sliced**
- **Salt and ground black pepper**
- **Spring salad mix, *Ready Pac*®**

1. Heat the bacon in microwave according to package directions.

2. Toast bread and spread each slice with blue cheese dressing. Place 4 slices of the bacon on half of the bread slices. Sprinkle with blue cheese. Top each sandwich with tomato slices and season to taste with salt and pepper. Add the lettuce and then the other piece of bread. Slice in half and serve.

Mexican Corn and Chicken Soup

Start to Finish 15 minutes **Makes** 4 servings

- 1 tablespoon canola oil
- ¾ cup frozen chopped onion, *Ore-Ida®*
- 2 teaspoons bottled garlic blend, *Gourmet Garden®*
- 1 teaspoon Mexican seasoning, *McCormick®*
- 2 tablespoons all-purpose flour
- 2 cans (14 ounces each) chicken broth, *Swanson®*
- 1 can (11-ounce) Mexicorn, *Green Giant®*
- 2 frozen mini corn on the cob, thawed and sliced into ½-inch pieces, *Green Giant® Nibblers*
- 1½ cups deli rotisserie chicken, skin removed, chopped
- 1 tablespoon heavy cream (optional)

1. In a large saucepan, heat oil over medium-high heat. Add onions, garlic, and Mexican seasoning; cook and stir 3 minutes. Add flour; cook and stir for 2 to 3 minutes or until flour starts to brown. Stir in chicken broth. Bring to a boil; reduce heat. Cover; simmer for 5 minutes. Stir in Mexicorn and corn on the cob; simmer 2 minutes.

2. Stir in chopped chicken; cook, uncovered, about 5 minutes or until corn is heated through. Remove from heat and stir in cream (optional). Serve hot.

Chicken Taco Wraps

Start to Finish 15 minutes **Makes** 4 servings

- 2 teaspoons taco seasoning mix, *McCormick®*
- ½ cup whipped cream cheese, *Philadelphia®*
- 4 soft taco-size tortillas, *Mission®*
- 4 tablespoons black bean and corn salsa, *Newman's Own®*
- 4 teaspoons diced green chiles, *Ortega®*
- 1 package (6-ounce) frozen cooked chicken breast strips, *Foster Farms®*
- 8 tablespoons shredded lettuce, *Fresh Express®*
- 4 tablespoons Mexican-style shredded cheese, *Kraft®*

1. In a small bowl, stir taco seasoning into cream cheese until well mixed. Spread 2 tablespoons of cream cheese mixture onto a tortilla. Top with 1 tablespoon of the salsa and 1 teaspoon of the green chiles. Add a few chicken strips and top with shredded lettuce and shredded cheese.

2. Tightly roll tortilla; cut in half. Repeat to make three more wraps.

Maw Maw's Crab and Corn Chowder

Start to Finish 15 minutes **Makes** 6 servings

- 1 **stick (½ cup) butter, cut into pieces**
- 1 **bag (12-ounce) frozen chopped onions, thawed, *Ore-Ida*®**
- 2 **cans (14.7 ounces each) creamed corn, *Green Giant*®**
- 1 **can (14.7-ounce) corn, drained, *Green Giant*®**
- 1 **can (10.75-ounce) condensed cream of potato soup, *Campbell's*®**
- 1 **cup half-and-half or light cream**
- 1 **cup reduced-sodium chicken broth, *Swanson*®**
- 1 **jar (4-ounce) pimientos, drained and chopped, *Dromedary*®**
- 1 **teaspoon celery seeds, crushed, *McCormick*®**
- 1 **bay leaf, *McCormick*®**
- 1 **container (16-ounce) canned crabmeat, *Blue Star*®**

1. In a large pot, melt butter over medium-high heat. Add onions; cook and stir until softened, but not browned. Stir in corn, condensed soup, half-and-half, broth, pimientos, celery seeds, and bay leaf until well mixed. Heat through, stirring often. Gently stir in crabmeat; heat through. Remove bay leaf before serving. Serve immediately.

Cajun Shrimp Salad Po'Boy

Prep 15 minutes **Chill** 1 hour **Makes** 4 servings

DRESSING

- ¾ **cup mayonnaise, *Best Foods*®/ *Hellmann's*®**
- 1 **tablespoon dried minced onions, *Spice Islands*®**
- 1½ **teaspoons Cajun seasoning, *McCormick*®**
- 1 **teaspoon stone-ground mustard, *Inglehoffer*®**

SHRIMP SALAD

- 1 **pound medium cooked, peeled shrimp, tails removed**
- ½ **cup frozen corn, thawed, *Green Giant*®**
- 1 **can (2.25-ounce) sliced black olives, drained, *Early California*®**
- 1 **jar (2-ounce) diced pimiento, drained, *Dromedary*®**
- ½ **cup chopped hard-cooked eggs, purchased from the salad bar**
- ¼ **cup finely chopped fresh flat-leaf parsley**
- 1 **tablespoon bottled garlic blend, *Gourmet Garden*®**
- 4 **French rolls, split lengthwise**
- 1 **lemon, cut into wedges (optional)**

1. For the dressing, in a medium bowl, stir together mayonnaise, onions, Cajun seasoning, and mustard; set aside.

2. For the shrimp salad, cut shrimp in half lengthwise; place in a large bowl. Add corn, olives, pimiento, eggs, parsley, and garlic; toss gently to combine. Pour dressing over shrimp and toss until well combined. Chill in refrigerator for 1 hour.

3. To serve, divide shrimp salad among split French rolls. Serve immediately with lemon wedges (optional).

Broccoli Cheese Soup

Start to Finish 20 minutes **Makes** 4 servings

- 2 tablespoons butter
- ¼ cup diced onions, *Ready Pac®*
- ¼ cup all-purpose flour
- 2 cups chicken broth, *Swanson®*
- 2 cups milk
- 12 ounces processed cheese, cut into small pieces, *Velveeta®*
- 1½ cups frozen chopped broccoli, thawed, *C & W®*
- Salt and ground black pepper

1. In a large saucepan, melt butter over medium-high heat. Add onions; cook and stir until tender. Stir in flour and cook about 5 minutes, stirring often. Stir in chicken broth and milk. Bring to a boil; reduce heat. Cook and stir for 3 to 4 minutes or until thickened, stirring occasionally. Stir in cheese; cook and stir until cheese melts. Stir in broccoli; heat through, stirring occasionally. Season to taste with salt and pepper. Serve hot.

Hot Turkey Smothered Sammich

Start to Finish 20 minutes **Makes** 4 servings

- 2 packets (1.6 ounces each) Alfredo sauce mix, *Knorr®*
- 2 cups milk
- 1 cup half-and-half or light cream
- ¾ cup grated Parmesan cheese, *DiGiorno®*
- 1 jar (2-ounce) diced pimientos, *Dromedary®*
- 8 slices fully cooked bacon, *Hormel®*
- 8 slices white bread, toasted and crusts trimmed off, *Sara Lee®*
- 1½ pounds deli turkey breast, thinly sliced

1. Preheat broiler to medium-high.

2. In a large saucepan, combine the sauce mix with the milk and cream. Bring to a gentle boil over medium heat, stirring constantly until the sauce thickens. Add ½ cup of the cheese and pimientos, stirring until well blended.

3. Heat the bacon in a microwave according to package directions. Meanwhile, for each sandwich, place 2 slices of the toasted bread on four broilerproof plates. Divide the turkey among the plates. Pour a generous amount of sauce over the turkey and sprinkle with 1 tablespoon of the remaining cheese per sandwich. Broil 4 inches from heat until the sauce is brown and bubbly. Remove from broiler and cross 2 slices of the bacon over the top of each sandwich, pressing down slightly. Serve immediately.

24 HOURS

Get-Well Chicken Soup

4-quart slow cooker **Prep** 10 minutes **Cook** 2 to 4 hours (high) or 6 to 8 hours (low) **Makes** 4 servings

- **½ of a deli rotisserie chicken**
- **2 cans (14 ounces each) reduced-sodium chicken broth, *Swanson*®**
- **1 can (10.75-ounce) condensed cream of mushroom soup with roasted garlic, *Campbell's*®**
- **1 cup carrot and celery sticks, diced, *Ready Pac*®**
- **½ cup diced onions, *Ready Pac*®**
- **1 teaspoon fines herbes blend, *McCormick*®**
- **Salt and ground black pepper**
- **1 cup uncooked egg noodles, *Manischewitz*®**

1. Remove skin from roasted chicken; remove meat from bones and shred meat. (Reserve other half of chicken for another use.)

2. In the slow cooker, stir together shredded chicken, chicken broth, mushroom soup, carrots and celery, onions, and fines herbes. Cover and cook on high setting for 2 to 4 hours or on low setting for 6 to 8 hours. Season to taste with salt and pepper.

3. Before serving, in a pot of boiling salted water, cook egg noodles according to package directions; drain. Stir egg noodles into soup to serve.

Grilled Cheese and Pesto

Start to Finish 15 minutes **Makes** 4 servings

- **8 slices cheddar cheese, *Kraft*®**
- **8 slices country potato bread, *Oroweat*®**
- **4 tablespoons refrigerated pesto sauce, *Buitoni*®**
- **8 slices sliced Swiss cheese, *Sargento*®**
- **Butter, softened**

1. Make a sandwich by laying 2 of the cheddar cheese slices on a slice of the potato bread. Top with 1 tablespoon of the pesto, 2 of the Swiss cheese slices, and another slice of potato bread. Repeat with remaining ingredients to make 4 sandwiches.

2. Heat a large skillet or griddle over medium to medium-low heat. Spread butter on one side of all sandwiches and place two sandwiches in skillet, butter sides down. Spread butter on the other sides of sandwiches once in pan. Cook about 6 minutes or until cheese is melted and bread is golden, turning once. Repeat with remaining sandwiches. Serve immediately.

Creamy Cauliflower Soup

Start to Finish 25 minutes **Makes** 4 servings

SOUP

- **1 tablespoon canola oil**
- **⅓ cup diced onions, *Ready Pac®***
- **2 teaspoons bottled garlic blend, *Gourmet Garden®***
- **3 cups frozen cauliflower, *Birds Eye®***
- **2 cups vegetable broth, *Swanson®***
- **1 can (10.75-ounce) condensed cream of potato soup, *Campbell's®***
- **1⅓ cups milk**
- **Salt and ground black pepper**

SALSA

- **1 cup packaged peeled baby carrots, coarsely chopped**
- **1 scallion (green onion), chopped (white and green parts)**
- **½ teaspoon bottled garlic blend, *Gourmet Garden®***
- **½ of a jalapeño chile, seeded and chopped**
- **Salt and ground black pepper**

1. For the soup, in a large saucepan, heat oil over medium-high heat. Add onions and garlic; cook and stir about 2 minutes or until onions are translucent. Add cauliflower, vegetable broth, and condensed soup. Bring to a boil; boil 8 to 10 minutes or until cauliflower is softened. Remove from heat; cool.

2. In a blender, combine cooled cauliflower mixture and milk. Cover and blend until smooth. Return to saucepan and heat through. Season to taste with salt and pepper. Clean blender.

3. For the salsa, in clean blender, combine carrots, scallion, garlic, and jalapeño. Pulse until coarsely chopped. Season to taste with salt and pepper.

4. To serve, top each serving of soup with salsa.

Mini Pepperoni Calzones

Prep 15 minutes **Bake** 15 minutes **Makes** 8 servings

- **Nonstick cooking spray, *Pam®***
- **1 tablespoon extra virgin olive oil**
- **⅓ cup diced onion, finely chopped, *Ready Pac®***
- **1 package (8-ounce) pepperoni, chopped, *Hormel®***
- **2 teaspoons bottled garlic blend, *Gourmet Garden®***
- **1 cup shredded 5-cheese Italian cheese blend, *Kraft®***
- **½ cup pizza sauce, *Prego®***
- **½ teaspoon Italian seasoning, *McCormick®***
- **Salt and ground black pepper**
- **1 roll (16.3-ounce) refrigerated biscuit dough, *Pillsbury®***
- **1 egg**
- **1 teaspoon water**

1. Preheat oven to 400°F. Spray a baking sheet with cooking spray; set aside.

2. For filling, in a medium skillet, heat oil over medium-high heat. Add onion; cook and stir about 3 minutes or until tender. Add pepperoni and garlic; cook for 4 minutes. Remove from heat; stir in cheese, pizza sauce, and Italian seasoning until well mixed. Season to taste with salt and pepper. Set aside to cool.

3. Open biscuit dough and separate dough into biscuits. On a lightly floured surface, roll each biscuit to a 6-inch circle. Divide filling mixture among dough circles. Combine egg and water; brush edges of dough with egg. Fold dough circles in half. Crimp edges of dough with a fork and transfer to prepared baking sheet. Pierce the top of each calzone with a fork and brush with egg and water mixture.

4. Bake for 15 to 20 minutes or until golden. Serve hot.

Easy Lobster Bisque

Start to Finish 30 minutes **Makes** 4 servings

- 2 (8 ounces each) frozen lobster tails, thawed and meat removed from shell
- 2 tablespoons extra virgin olive oil
- 1 medium yellow onion, minced
- 2 cups milk
- 1½ cups heavy cream
- 2 tablespoons butter
- 1 can (10-ounce) condensed cream of shrimp soup, *Campbell's®*
- 1 can (10.75-ounce) condensed cream of mushroom soup, *Campbell's®*
- ¼ teaspoon cayenne pepper, *McCormick®*
- ½ teaspoon celery seeds, *McCormick®*
- ¼ cup dry sherry, *Christian Brothers®*
- Fresh dill sprigs (optional)

1. Place the tail shells in a zip-top bag. Hit with a rubber mallet to break up.

2. In a medium saucepan, heat olive oil over medium-high heat. Add the lobster tail shells and onion; cook and stir for 6 to 8 minutes or until onion softens. Add milk and cream; simmer for 15 minutes. Remove from heat and cool slightly. Strain milk mixture to remove lobster shells; discard shells.

3. Coarsely chop the lobster tail meat. In a large saucepan, melt the butter over medium heat. Add the lobster meat. Cook and stir for 5 to 6 minutes or until the lobster is opaque. Reduce heat; add the condensed soups, cayenne pepper, and celery seeds. Add the strained milk mixture, stirring until blended. Simmer about 5 minutes or until heated through, stirring occasionally.

4. Ladle soup into 4 soup bowls, dividing the lobster meat into each bowl. Drizzle each bowl with 1 tablespoon sherry and top with a dill sprig (optional).

Crab Cake Sliders

Prep 15 minutes **Bake** 8 minutes **Makes** 4 servings

CAJUN TARTAR SAUCE

- 1 bottle (10-ounce) tartar sauce, *Best Foods®/Hellmann's®*
- 2 teaspoons Cajun seasoning, *McCormick®*
- 1 scallion (green onion), finely chopped
- 6 dashes hot pepper sauce, *Tabasco®*

CRAB CAKES

- 2 cans (6 ounces each) lump crabmeat, drained, *Crown Prince®*
- 1 cup fresh bread crumbs
- 1 tablespoon fines herbes blend, *McCormick®*
- 1 box (8.5-ounce) corn muffin mix, *Jiffy®*
- Vegetable oil for frying
- 12 sweet buns, *King's Hawaiian®*
- Butter lettuce leaves
- Tomatoes, sliced

1. Preheat oven to 375°F.

2. For Cajun tartar sauce, in a small bowl, stir together tartar sauce, Cajun seasoning, scallion, and hot pepper sauce.

3. For crab cakes, in a medium bowl, stir together drained crab meat and 1 cup of the Cajun Tartar Sauce until mixed. Add bread crumbs and fines herbes; toss just until combined. (Overmixing will cause crab cakes to become gummy.) Form mixture into about twelve 2-inch crab cakes.

4. Pour corn muffin mix into a shallow dish. Carefully dredge crab cakes in corn muffin mix; set aside.

5. In a large skillet, add enough oil to cover bottom; heat oil over medium heat. When oil is shimmering, fry crab cakes in batches about 2 minutes per side or just until golden. Transfer to a baking sheet.

6. Bake for 8 to 10 minutes or until heated through. Serve crab cakes on sweet buns with lettuce, tomato, and additional Cajun tartar sauce.

Hot and Sour Soup

Start to Finish 15 minutes **Makes** 4 servings

- 2½ cups water
- 1 bottle (12-ounce) clam juice, *Snow's®*
- 1 lime, peel grated and juice reserved
- 3 tablespoons lime juice, *ReaLime®*
- 1 can (8 ounces drained weight) straw mushrooms, drained
- 1 small tomato, peeled and cut into thin wedges
- 1 tablespoon minced lemongrass, *Gourmet Garden®*
- 1 teaspoon chili-garlic sauce, *Lee Kum Kee®*
- 12 ounces medium shrimp, peeled and deveined
- 4 ounces fresh shiitake mushrooms, stemmed and caps thinly sliced
- ½ teaspoon salt
- 2 scallions (green onions), diagonally sliced
- 2 tablespoons dry sherry, *Christian Brothers®*

1. In a large pot, combine the water, clam juice, grated lime peel, lime juice, and bottled lime juice; bring to a boil. Add straw mushrooms, tomato, lemongrass, and chili-garlic sauce. Return to a boil; reduce heat to medium. Simmer 5 minutes.

2. Add the shrimp, shiitakes, and salt; simmer for 2 more minutes. Stir in scallions and sherry before serving. Serve hot.

Chicken Lettuce Wraps

Start to Finish 15 minutes **Makes** 4 servings

- 1 tablespoon vegetable oil
- 1½ pounds uncooked ground chicken
- 1 teaspoon salt
- ½ teaspoon ground black pepper
- ¾ cup diced onions, finely chopped, *Ready Pac®*
- ½ cup peanuts, *Planters®*
- ¼ cup spicy Thai chile sauce, *Thai Kitchen®*
- 4 teaspoons lime juice, *ReaLime®*
- ¼ cup finely chopped fresh cilantro
- 1 head butterhead (Boston or Bibb) lettuce, rinsed and patted dry

1. In a large skillet, heat vegetable oil over medium-high heat. When oil is shimmering, add ground chicken, salt, and pepper. Cook chicken until cooked through, using a spatula to break into small pieces. Add chopped onions; cook and stir about 2 minutes or until onions are soft. Stir in peanuts, chile sauce, and lime juice. Heat through, stirring occasionally. Remove from heat and stir in cilantro.

2. To serve, form a single lettuce leaf into a cup and spoon 2 tablespoons of the chicken mixture into lettuce cup. Repeat with remaining lettuce leaves and chicken mixture.

French Onion Soup

4-quart slow cooker **Cook** 4 hours (high) or 8 hours (low) **Makes** 8 servings

- **5** cups onions, sliced
- **2** cans (14 ounces each) reduced-sodium beef broth, ***Swanson***®
- **2** cans (10 ounces each) beef consommé, ***Campbell's***®
- **1** envelope onion soup mix, ***Lipton***®
- **8** slices French bread
- **1** cup shredded Gruyère cheese

1. In the slow cooker, combine onions, broth, consommé, and soup mix. Cook on high for 4 hours or on low for 8 hours.

2. Ladle soup into broilerproof serving bowls. Top each with a slice of French bread. Sprinkle 2 tablespoons of the cheese over each bread slice. Broil soup 4 to 6 inches from heat until cheese melts.

Barbecue Belt Beef Sandwich

Start to Finish 20 minutes **Makes** 4 servings

- **1** bottle (12-ounce) chili sauce, ***Heinz***®
- **1** cup beer, ***Budweiser***®
- **¼** cup molasses, ***Grandma's***®
- **1** packet (1.31-ounce) sloppy joe seasoning mix, ***McCormick***®
- **2** tablespoons packed brown sugar
- **12** slices cooked beef brisket
- **1** box (11.25-ounce) garlic Texas toast, ***Pepperidge Farm***®

1. Preheat oven to 425°F.

2. In a large skillet, stir together chili sauce, beer, molasses, sloppy joe mix, and brown sugar. Bring to a boil; reduce heat. Simmer for 10 minutes, stirring frequently. Add sliced brisket and simmer for 3 to 4 minutes or until beef is heated through.

3. Meanwhile, arrange Texas toast, spread sides up, on a baking sheet. Bake for 5 to 6 minutes or until heated through.

4. To assemble each sandwich, arrange 3 slices of the brisket on each piece of toast. Spoon some sauce over and top with another slice of toast.

Creamy Artichoke Soup

Prep 5 minutes **Cook** 10 minutes **Makes** 4 servings

- 1 **can (14-ounce) reduced-sodium chicken broth,** ***Swanson®***
- 1 **can (10.75-ounce) condensed cream of celery soup,** ***Campbell's®***
- 1 **jar (12-ounce) artichoke hearts (water pack), drained,** ***Cara Mia®***
- **Dash cayenne pepper,** ***McCormick®***
- ½ **cup half-and-half or light cream**
- **Salt and ground black pepper**

1. In a blender, combine chicken broth, celery soup, and artichoke hearts; process until smooth.

2. Pour mixture into a medium saucepan and heat over medium-high heat. Add cayenne pepper. Bring to a boil; reduce heat. Simmer for 10 minutes. Stir in cream and season to taste with salt and black pepper.

Hot Italian Grinder

Start to Finish 25 minutes **Makes** 6 servings

- 1 **package (16-ounce) hot Italian sausage,** ***Papa Cantella's®***
- 1 **loaf Italian or sourdough bread, sliced in half horizontally**
- 4 **tablespoons (or more) balsamic vinaigrette,** ***Newman's Own®***
- 2 **cups shredded iceberg lettuce**
- 4 **ounces thinly sliced Genoa salami, from deli**
- 4 **ounces thinly sliced pastrami, from deli**
- 4 **ounces thinly sliced mortadella, from deli**
- 4 **ounces thinly sliced mozzarella cheese, from deli**
- 4 **ounces thinly sliced provolone cheese, from deli**
- 1 **large tomato, thinly sliced**
- 1 **red onion, thinly sliced**
- ¼ **cup olive bruschetta topping,** ***DeLallo®***
- ¼ **cup shredded Parmesan cheese,** ***DiGiorno®***
- **Crushed red pepper (optional),** ***McCormick®***

1. Set up grill for direct cooking over medium heat. Oil grate when ready to start cooking. Prick sausages with a fork and place on hot oiled grill. Cook for 10 to 15 minutes or until an instant-read thermometer inserted in center of each sausage registers 160°F, turning frequently.

2. Halve sausages lengthwise and grill, cut sides down, about 1 minute more or until sausages are browned. Remove to platter; cover and keep warm.

3. Drizzle cut sides of bread with 2 tablespoons of the vinaigrette; grill, cut sides down, until toasted.

4. In a medium bowl, toss lettuce with remaining 2 tablespoons vinaigrette; spoon over bottom half of bread loaf. Layer grilled sausages, deli meats, cheeses, tomato, and onion on lettuce. Sprinkle with olive bruschetta topping, Parmesan, and crushed red pepper (optional). Place top of bread loaf on sandwich. Cut into serving-size sandwiches.

Indoor Method: In a large skillet, cover sausages with water. Bring to a simmer over medium heat; cook about 10 minutes or until almost cooked through. Remove sausages with a slotted spoon. Preheat broiler. Place partially cooked sausages on a wire rack over a foil-lined baking sheet or broiler pan. Broil 6 to 8 inches from heat for 8 to 12 minutes or until an instant-read thermometer inserted in center of each sausage registers 160°F. Remove and halve sausages lengthwise and broil for 1 minute more, cut sides up. Assemble sandwich as directed.

Perfect Potato Leek Soup

Start to Finish 25 minutes **Makes** 4 servings

- 2 **tablespoons butter**
- 2 **large leeks, white parts only, well washed and chopped**
- 1 **teaspoon bottled crushed garlic, *Gourmet Garden*®**
- 1 **bag (24-ounce) frozen cut russet potatoes, *Ore-Ida*® *Steam n' Mash*®**
- 4 **cups reduced-sodium chicken broth, *Swanson*®**
- ½ **cup light cream or milk**
- **Salt and ground black pepper**
- **Finely chopped fresh chives (optional)**

1. In a large saucepan or soup pot, melt butter over medium-high heat. Add leeks and garlic; cook and stir about 5 minutes or until tender. Add frozen potatoes and chicken broth. Bring to a boil; reduce heat. Simmer for 15 minutes. Remove from heat and cool.

2. Transfer mixture to a blender (work in batches if necessary). Cover and puree until smooth. (Soup can be stored in refrigerator up to two days at this point.) Stir in cream; season to taste with salt and pepper. Top with chives (optional).

Grilled Corned Beef Sandwich

Start to Finish 20 minutes **Makes** 4 servings

- 2 **tablespoons prepared horseradish sauce, *Kraft*®**
- 1 **tablespoon yellow mustard, *French's*®**
- **Nonstick cooking spray, *Pam*®**
- 1 **box (11.25-ounce) frozen Texas Toast, *Pepperidge Farm*® *Garlic***
- 8 **ounces sliced corned beef, from deli**
- 8 **slices Gouda cheese, *Sargento*®**
- **Kosher dill pickles, *Claussen*® (optional)**

1. In a small bowl, stir together horseradish sauce and mustard until well mixed; set aside.

2. Spray a large grill pan with cooking spray; heat pan over medium-high. Place Texas Toast on grill pan and grill for 2 minutes. Remove toast slices from pan with metal spatula.

3. Heat corned beef slices on a large microwave-safe plate on high for 30 seconds. Remove, cover, and set aside.

4. Spread 1 teaspoon of the horseradish-mustard mixture on each of the grilled sides of the toast. Top each with a slice of cheese and warm corned beef. Make sandwiches by combining 2 toasts topped with cheese and corned beef so corned beef is in the middle of the sandwich and ungrilled sides of toasts are on the outside of sandwich. Place each sandwich in heated pan and grill about 4 minutes or until cheese has melted and toast is golden, turning once. Remove and serve immediately with dill pickles (optional).

Stews & Chilies

A big pot of stew simmering on the stove fills the house with mouthwatering aromas and holds the promise of something wonderful to eat. Hearty and warming, stews and chilies are terrific for casual entertaining. They can bubble away on the stovetop and guests can help themselves to as many bowls—and fixings—as they like.

NCHOR BREWING CO
BERTY AL
SAN FRANCISC
Hot

Salisbury Steak Stew

Prep 20 minutes **Cook** 35 minutes **Makes** 6 servings

- 1 **tablespoon all-purpose flour**
- 1¼ **pounds ground beef sirloin**
- ¼ **cup garlic and herb seasoned coating mix, *Shake 'N Bake*®**
- 1 **tablespoon Worcestershire sauce, *Lea & Perrins*®**
- 1 **teaspoon bottled crushed garlic, *Gourmet Garden*®**
- 3 **tablespoons extra virgin olive oil**
- 1 **large onion, roughly chopped**
- 2 **tablespoons packed brown sugar, *C&H*®**
- 1 **can (10.75-ounce) condensed cream of mushroom with roasted garlic soup, *Campbell's*®**
- ¾ **cup beef broth, *Swanson*®**
- ½ **cup beef gravy, *Heinz*®**
- 1 **teaspoon ground thyme, *McCormick*®**
- 1 **tablespoon dry sherry, *Christian Brothers*®**
- 1½ **tablespoons tomato paste, *Contadina*®**
- **Parsley sprigs (optional)**

1. Place flour in a shallow pie plate; set aside. In a large bowl, combine ground beef, coating mix, Worcestershire sauce, and crushed garlic until well mixed. Shape into 18 to 20 oval-shape patties. Dip each beef patty in flour, turning to coat evenly.

2. In a large saucepan, heat 1 tablespoon of the oil over medium-high heat. Brown patties on all sides in hot oil; use tongs to transfer patties to a plate. Cover with foil; set aside.

3. In the same saucepan, heat the remaining 2 tablespoons oil over high heat. Add onion and cook for 5 minutes, stirring occasionally. Sprinkle brown sugar over onion; cook about 15 minutes more or until caramelized, stirring often.

4. Meanwhile, in a medium bowl, stir together mushroom soup, beef broth, gravy, and thyme; set aside.

5. Pour sherry into onions and deglaze pan by scraping bits from bottom of pan. Stir in tomato paste. Pour in soup-gravy mixture. Bring to a boil; reduce heat to medium-low. Return meat to pan. Cover and cook about 10 minutes or until heated through. Serve hot with parsley sprig on each serving (optional).

Lone Star Chili

Prep 15 minutes **Cook** 1 hour **Makes** 4 servings

CHILI

- 1½ **pounds top sirloin steak or stew meat, cut into ½-inch or smaller cubes**
- 1 **teaspoon salt**
- 1 **teaspoon ground ancho chile pepper, *McCormick® Gourmet Collection***
- 2 **tablespoons canola oil or bacon grease**
- 1½ **cups frozen chopped onions, thawed, *Ore-Ida®***
- 1 **can (7-ounce) diced green chile peppers, *Ortega®***
- 1 **tablespoon bottled chopped garlic, *Gourmet Garden®***
- 1 **can (14-ounce) reduced-sodium beef broth, *Swanson®***
- 1 **can (10.75-ounce) tomato puree, *Hunt's®***
- ¾ **cup Texas beer, *Shiner Bock®***
- 1 **package Tex-Mex chili seasoning mix, *McCormick®***

TOPPINGS

Shredded sharp cheddar cheese, *Sargento®*

Diced onion

Sour cream

Saltine or cornbread crackers

1. In a medium bowl, toss the beef with salt and ground ancho chile. In a medium pot, heat oil or bacon grease over medium-high heat. Add beef, onions, chiles, and garlic; cook until beef is browned, stirring often. Stir in beef broth, tomato puree, beer, and seasoning mix; Bring to a boil. Reduce heat to low; cover and simmer for 1 to 1½ hours, stirring occasionally.

2. Ladle chili into bowls and serve with cheese, diced onion, sour cream, and crackers.

Chili in a Pepper

Prep 25 minutes **Bake** 50 minutes **Makes** 4 servings

- **4** **large red, yellow, and/or orange bell peppers**
- **1** **pound lean ground beef**
- **1** **container (5-ounce) diced onions, *Ready Pac*®**
- **½** **teaspoon salt**
- **¼** **teaspoon ground black pepper**
- **1** **can (15-ounce) pinto beans, drained, *S&W*®**
- **¼** **cup diced green chiles, *Ortega*®**
- **½** **cup tomato sauce, *Contadina*®**
- **1** **packet (1.31-ounce) sloppy joe seasoning mix, *McCormick*®**
- **2** **tablespoons hot pepper sauce or to taste, *Tabasco*®**
- **1** **teaspoon ground cumin, *McCormick*®**
- **1** **teaspoon chili powder, *McCormick*®**
- **2** **tablespoons vegetable oil**
- **Sour cream (optional)**

1. Preheat oven to 350°F.

2. Remove a slice off the top of each bell pepper; set tops aside. Remove seeds and membranes from center of each bell pepper. Arrange bell peppers in a baking dish, sitting upright. (Trim bottoms of peppers, if necessary, to sit upright.)

3. In a large skillet, brown ground beef and onions over medium-high heat about 5 minutes or until meat is no longer pink. Using a slotted spoon, transfer beef to a medium bowl; stir in salt and pepper. Stir in beans and green chiles until well mixed. In a small bowl, stir together tomato sauce, sloppy joe seasoning mix, hot pepper sauce, cumin, and chili powder until well mixed. Pour tomato sauce mixture over meat mixture and mix well.

4. Fill each bell pepper with meat mixture and top with reserved pepper tops. Using a pastry brush, coat each bell pepper with oil.

5. Bake for 50 to 60 minutes or until filling is heated through and bell peppers are tender. Serve hot with a scoop of sour cream (optional).

Note: For a vegetarian option, substitute another 15-ounce can pinto beans for the ground beef.

Bacon, Portobello, and Wild Rice Stew

Start to Finish 18 minutes **Makes** 6 servings

- 2 tablespoons extra virgin olive oil
- 2 packages (6 ounces each) sliced portobello mushrooms, cut into 1-inch pieces
- 1 teaspoon bottled crushed garlic, *Gourmet Garden®*
- 2 tablespoons dry sherry, *Christian Brothers®*
- 1 can (14-ounce) beef broth, *Swanson®*
- 1 cup water
- ¾ cup mushroom gravy, *Heinz® Home Style*
- 1 box (6.2-ounce) fast-cooking long grain and wild rice, *Uncle Ben's®*
- ¾ cup crumbled real bacon, *Hormel®*
- Chopped fresh flat-leaf parsley (optional)

1. In a large saucepan, heat oil over medium-high heat. Add mushrooms and garlic; cook and stir for 3 minutes. Add sherry and deglaze pan by scraping bits from bottom of pan. Add beef broth, water, and mushroom gravy. Bring to a boil. Add rice with seasoning packet and bacon; return to a boil. Cover; reduce heat to low and simmer for 6 to 8 minutes.

2. Remove from heat and let stand, covered, for 5 minutes. Serve hot with chopped parsley (optional).

Couscous Paella

Prep 10 minutes **Cook** 5 minutes **Makes** 8 servings

- 1 **teaspoon extra virgin olive oil**
- 1 **container (5-ounce) diced onions, *Ready Pac*®**
- 1 **teaspoon bottled crushed garlic, *Gourmet Garden*®**
- 1 **cup sliced Andouille sausage, *Aidells*®**
- 1 **can (14.5-ounce) diced tomatoes, *Muir Glen*®**
- 1½ **cups frozen petite peas with pearl onions, *C&W*®**
- 1 **can (14-ounce) vegetable stock, *Swanson*®**
- 1 **tablespoon frozen lemon juice, thawed, *Minute Maid*®**
- ½ **teaspoon red pepper flakes, *McCormick*®**
- **Pinch saffron threads, *McCormick*®**
- 1 **box (10-ounce) couscous mix, *Near East*®**
- 1½ **cups frozen medium cooked shrimp without tails, thawed, *Contessa*®**
- **Salt and ground black pepper**

1. In a large skillet, heat oil over medium-high heat. Add onions and garlic; cook and stir for 2 minutes. Add sausage and cook for 1 minute. Add tomatoes and peas and cook for 2 minutes. Add vegetable stock, lemon juice, red pepper flakes, and saffron.

2. Bring to a boil; remove from heat. Stir in couscous mix and shrimp. Cover and let stand for 5 to 7 minutes or until couscous absorbs all liquid. Season to taste with salt and pepper. Serve warm.

Italian Sausage Stew

Start to Finish 25 minutes **Makes** 8 servings

- 2 packages (9 ounces each) fresh plain or spinach fettuccine, *Buitoni*®
- 2 tablespoons extra virgin olive oil
- 1 package (12-ounce) artichoke and garlic sausage, *Aidells*®
- 1 cup frozen chopped onions, *Ore-Ida*®
- 2 teaspoons bottled chopped garlic, *Gourmet Garden*®
- 1 cup vegetable broth, *Swanson*®
- 1 jar (26-ounce) tomato, basil, and garlic pasta sauce, *Prego*®
- 1 can (14.5-ounce) Italian stewed tomatoes, *Del Monte*®
- 1 medium turnip, peeled and diced
- 1 bag (8-ounce) cleaned and trimmed Brussels sprouts
- 2 cups petite broccoli florets, from salad bar

1. In a large pot of boiling salted water, cook fettuccine according to package directions. Drain; cover to keep warm.

2. While pasta cooks, in a large saucepan, heat oil over medium-high heat. Add sausage; cook about 5 minutes or until browned on all sides. Transfer sausage to a plate; cover and set aside.

3. Add onions and garlic to pan; cook and stir for 2 minutes. Add vegetable broth and deglaze pan by scraping bits from bottom of pan. Add pasta sauce, stewed tomatoes, and turnip. Bring to a boil.

4. Make an "x" with a sharp knife on the bottom of each Brussels sprout; add to saucepan. Reduce heat, cover, and simmer for 10 minutes. Add broccoli and simmer, uncovered, for 10 minutes more.

5. Cut sausage into ½-inch slices and return to sauce in pan. Heat through. Serve sauce over fettuccine.

Barbeque Pork Chili

Prep 10 minutes **Cook** 30 minutes **Makes** 6 servings

- 1 **tablespoon canola oil**
- 1 **cup frozen chopped onions, *Ore-Ida®***
- 1 **container (18-ounce) barbecue shredded pork, *Lloyd's®***
- 1 **tablespoon bottled garlic blend, *Gourmet Garden®***
- 2 **cans (16 ounces each) pinto beans, drained, *Bush's®***
- 2 **cans (10 ounces each) diced tomatoes and green chiles, *Ro-Tel®***
- 1 **cup beer, *Budweiser®***
- ½ **cup barbecue sauce, *Bull's-Eye®***
- 2 **tablespoons diced jalapeño, *La Victoria®***
- 1 **teaspoon ground cumin, *McCormick®***
- ½ **teaspoon chili powder, *McCormick®***

1. In a large pot, heat oil over medium heat. Add onions; cook and stir until tender. Add shredded pork and garlic; cook about 2 minutes or just until heated through.

2. Stir in beans, tomatoes, beer, barbecue sauce, jalapeño, cumin, and chili powder until well mixed. Bring to a boil; reduce heat. Simmer for 30 to 45 minutes or until desired consistency, stirring occasionally. Serve hot.

Chicken Stew with Fennel and Mushrooms

Prep 20 minutes **Cook** 45 minutes **Makes** 4 servings

- **3 large boneless, skinless chicken breasts**
- **1 teaspoon salt**
- **1 teaspoon ground black pepper**
- **2 tablespoons extra virgin olive oil**
- **1½ cups frozen chopped onions, *Ore-Ida*®**
- **1 cup frozen sliced carrots, *Birds Eye*®**
- **2 fennel bulbs, trimmed and thinly sliced lengthwise (reserve fronds)**
- **1 cup dry white wine or chicken broth**
- **4 cups reduced-sodium chicken broth, *Swanson*®**
- **1 can (10.75-ounce) condensed cream of mushroom soup, *Campbell's*®**
- **1 package (8-ounce) sliced brown mushrooms**
- **1 tablespoon bottled garlic blend, *Gourmet Garden*®**
- **Salt and ground black pepper**

1. Cut chicken into bite-size pieces and sprinkle with the 1 teaspoon salt and 1 teaspoon pepper. In a large pot or Dutch oven, heat the oil over medium-high. Add chicken; cook and stir about 3 minutes or until brown. Transfer chicken to a plate.

2. Add the onions, carrots, and sliced fennel to the pot; cook for 5 to 6 minutes or until vegetables are softened and lightly browned, stirring constantly. Add wine and deglaze pot by scraping bits from bottom of pan. Stir in the 4 cups chicken broth, mushroom soup, mushrooms, and garlic until well mixed. Add the chicken and any accumulated juices on plate back to the pot.

3. Bring to a boil; reduce heat to low. Cover and simmer on low for 45 to 50 minutes. Season to taste with salt and pepper before serving. Serve with reserved fennel fronds (optional).

Turkey Stew with Puffed Lids

5-quart slow cooker **Prep** 5 minutes **Cook** 4 to 5 hours (high) **Makes** 8 servings

TURKEY STEW

- 2 cans (10 ounces each) condensed cream of chicken soup, *Campbell's®*
- 1 to 2 cups water
- 2 teaspoons salt-free chicken seasoning, *McCormick® Grill Mates®*
- 1½ to 2 pounds turkey cutlets, cut into bite-size pieces
- 1 package (16-ounce) frozen mixed vegetables, *C&W®*
- 2 large red potatoes, diced
- 1 medium yellow onion, chopped

PASTRY LIDS

- 1 sheet frozen puff pastry (half of a 17.3-ounce package), thawed in refrigerator, *Pepperidge Farm®*
- 1 egg
- 1 teaspoon water

1. For the stew, in the slow cooker, stir together soup, water, and chicken seasoning. Add turkey, mixed vegetables, potatoes, and onion; mix well. Cover and cook on high for 4 to 5 hours.

2. For the pastry lids, preheat oven to 400°F about 30 minutes before turkey mixture is done. Unfold thawed pastry; using a fluted pastry wheel or sharp knife, cut dough into three pieces along fold marks. Cut each piece into thirds to make 9 dough pieces total. Place dough on an ungreased baking sheet, about 1 inch apart. Stir together egg and water; brush on dough, being careful not to drip egg on baking sheet. Bake about 20 minutes or until puffed and golden.

3. To serve, ladle hot turkey mixture into bowls and top with puffed pastry lids.

Turkey Taco Chili

Prep 10 minutes **Cook** 35 minutes **Makes** 6 servings

- 2 **pounds turkey cutlets, cut into bite-size pieces**
- 1 **packet (1.25-ounce) taco seasoning, *McCormick*®**
- 2 **tablespoons canola oil**
- ¾ **cup diced onion, *Ready Pac*®**
- 1 **can (10-ounce) diced tomatoes and green chiles, *Ro-Tel*®**
- 1 **can (8-ounce) tomato sauce, *Contadina*®**
- ¾ **cup chicken broth, *Swanson*®**
- ½ **cup red taco sauce, *La Victoria*®**
- 2 **teaspoons garlic salt, *McCormick*®**
- 1 **can (15-ounce) kidney beans, drained, *S&W*®**
- 1 **can (16-ounce) pinto beans, drained, *Bush's*®**
- **Salt and ground black pepper**
- 1½ **cups shredded cheddar cheese, *Kraft*®**
- **Fresh cilantro leaves**
- **Crushed tortilla chips (optional)**

1. Season turkey cutlets with taco seasoning; set aside.

2. In a large pot, heat oil over medium heat. Add onion; cook and stir until tender. Add turkey pieces. Cook about 5 minutes or until cooked through. In a large bowl, stir together diced tomatoes, tomato sauce, chicken broth, taco sauce, and garlic salt; pour into pot. Add beans. Bring to a boil; reduce heat. Simmer for 30 to 45 minutes, stirring occasionally.

3. To serve, season chili to taste with salt and pepper. Top each serving with shredded cheese and cilantro. Serve hot with crushed tortilla chips (optional).

Sides

Whether it's a creamy vegetable casserole, wholesome grain salad, cheesy pasta or rice, or a mound of light and fluffy whipped potatoes—side dishes turn a main dish into a full meal. Pairing any of these homey sides with a main course such as ham, roast chicken, steak, or chops makes the simplest meal special.

Zucchini Casserole

Prep 12 minutes **Bake** 30 minutes **Makes** 4 servings

- **Nonstick cooking spray, *Pam*®**
- ¼ **cup unsalted butter, melted**
- 2 **tablespoons olive oil**
- 1 **cup diced onions, *Ready Pac*®**
- 2 **pounds zucchini, sliced ¼ inch thick**
- 3 **eggs**
- 1 **can (5-ounce) evaporated milk, *Carnation*®**
- 1 **cup grated Parmigiano Reggiano cheese**
- 2 **tablespoons bread crumbs, *Progresso*®**
- **Red pepper flakes (about ½ teaspoon), *McCormick*®**
- 1 **teaspoon kosher salt**
- 1 **teaspoon lemon pepper, *McCormick*®**
- ¼ **teaspoon ground black pepper**

1. Preheat oven to 350°F. Spray a 9×13-inch baking dish with cooking spray; set aside.

2. In a large skillet, melt butter with olive oil over medium-high heat. Add onions and zucchini. Reduce heat to medium. Cover and cook for 5 to 7 minutes or until onions are softened, stirring occasionally. Remove from heat and set aside.

3. In a medium bowl, stir together eggs and evaporated milk. Stir in ½ cup of the cheese, bread crumbs, pepper flakes, salt, lemon pepper, and black pepper. Stir in zucchini-onion mixture. Transfer to prepared baking dish. Sprinkle with remaining cheese.

4. Bake for 30 to 35 minutes or until a light golden.

Pumpkin Pie-Spiced Sweet Potatoes

Prep 5 minutes **Bake** 30 minutes **Makes** 4 servings

- **Nonstick cooking spray, *Pam*®**
- **1 can (29-ounce) cut sweet potatoes, drained, *Princella*®**
- **1 cup golden raisins, *Sun-Maid*®**
- **½ cup packed brown sugar, *C&H*®**
- **2 teaspoons curry powder, *McCormick*®**
- **2 teaspoons pumpkin pie spice, *McCormick*®**
- **½ teaspoon salt**
- **¼ cup sliced almonds or pistachios, *Planters*®**
- **2 tablespoons butter**

1. Preheat oven to 350°F. Lightly spray a 1-quart casserole dish with cooking spray; set aside.

2. In a large bowl, combine sweet potatoes and golden raisins; set aside.

3. In a small bowl, combine brown sugar, curry powder, pumpkin pie spice, and salt. Stir into sweet potatoes until well mixed. Transfer to prepared casserole dish. Top with sliced almonds or pistachios and dot with butter. Bake for 30 minutes.

Sweet Potato and Rice Soufflé

Prep 10 minutes **Bake** 35 minutes **Makes** 6 servings

- 1 **bag (24-ounce) frozen cut sweet potatoes, *Ore-Ida® Steam n' Mash®***
- 2 **packages (8.8 ounces each) precooked buttery rice, *Uncle Ben's® Ready Rice***
- 2 **cans (8 ounces each) crushed pineapple, *Dole®***
- 2 **eggs, lightly beaten**
- 1 **cup half-and-half**
- 2 **tablespoons packed dark brown sugar, *C&H®***
- 1 **teaspoon pumpkin pie spice, *McCormick®***
- 1 **teaspoon kosher salt**
- ½ **teaspoon ground black pepper**
- ¼ **cup pecans, coarsely chopped, *Planters®***

1. Preheat oven to 350°F. Lightly spray a 1½-quart soufflé dish or six 2-cup individual soufflé dishes with cooking spray.

2. In a microwave, cook sweet potatoes and rice separately according to package directions. Do not mash sweet potatoes. Layer half of the sweet potatoes, 1 can of pineapple, and 1 package of rice in prepared dish(es). Repeat layering.

3. In a medium bowl, stir together eggs, half-and-half, brown sugar, pumpkin pie spice, salt, and pepper; pour over casserole(s).

4. Bake for 25 minutes; sprinkle pecans over top of casserole(s). Bake for 10 to 15 minutes more (5 minutes for individual soufflés) or until slightly puffed. Serve immediately.

Bulgur Pilaf with Vegetables

Prep 20 minutes **Stand** 20 minutes **Makes** 5 servings

- 3 tablespoons butter
- 1 cup frozen onions, *Ore-Ida®*
- 1 teaspoon bottled crushed garlic, *Gourmet Garden®*
- 2 cups frozen vegetable medley, thawed, *C & W® Ultimate Tuscan Blend*
- 1 box (5.25-ounce) wheat bulgur mix (2 teaspoons of herb packet reserved), *Near East®*
- 1 cup chicken stock, *Swanson®*
- ¼ cup sliced almonds, *Planters®*
- Salt and ground black pepper

1. Preheat oven to 350°F. Line a baking sheet with foil; set aside.

2. In a medium skillet, melt butter over medium-high heat. Add onions and garlic. Cook for 2 minutes. Add vegetable medley and cook for 2 minutes. Add bulgur mix with 2 teaspoons of the herb packet and cook for 1 minute. Add chicken stock. Bring to a boil; remove from heat. Cover and let stand for 20 minutes or until liquid is absorbed.

3. Meanwhile, spread an even layer of almonds on prepared baking sheet. Bake for 8 to 10 minutes or until nuts are fragrant and golden, stirring once. Stir toasted almonds into pilaf. Season to taste with salt and pepper. Serve hot.

Black Bean and Rice Bake

Prep 15 minutes **Bake** 30 minutes **Makes** 5 servings

- **Nonstick cooking spray, *Pam*®**
- 2 **cups reduced-sodium chicken broth, *Swanson*®**
- 1 **package (5.6-ounce) Spanish rice mix, *Lipton® Fiesta Sides***
- 1 **tablespoon extra virgin olive oil**
- 3 **cups frozen yellow and green zucchini squash, thawed, *C & W*®**
- 1 **can (10-ounce) diced tomatoes and green chiles, drained, *Ro-Tel*®**
- 1 **tablespoon fajita seasoning, *McCormick*®**
- **Salt and ground black pepper**
- 1 **can (16-ounce) refried black beans, *Rosarita*®**
- 1½ **cups shredded 4-cheese Mexican cheese blend, *Sargento*®**

1. Preheat oven to 350°F. Spray a 1½-quart casserole dish with cooking spray; set aside.

2. In a medium saucepan, combine broth, rice mix, and olive oil. Bring to a boil; reduce heat. Cover and simmer for 6 to 8 minutes or until all liquid is absorbed. Remove from heat.

3. Meanwhile, in a medium bowl, stir together squash, diced tomatoes, and fajita seasoning. Season to taste with salt and pepper; set aside.

4. Spread beans in bottom of prepared casserole dish and top with ¾ cup of the cheese. Spoon half of the squash mixture over cheese. Top with cooked rice. Spoon remaining squash mixture over top and sprinkle with remaining ¾ cup cheese.

5. Bake for 30 to 35 minutes or until heated through. Serve warm.

Brew-Baked Beans

Prep 20 minutes **Bake** 45 minutes **Makes** 8 servings

- 4 **ounces bacon, chopped, *Farmer John®***
- 1 **medium red onion, diced**
- 2 **cans (28 ounces each) baked beans, *Bush's® Original***
- 1 **bottle (12-ounce) lager-style beer**
- ¼ **cup ketchup, *Heinz®***
- ¼ **cup spicy brown mustard, *Gulden's®***
- 3 **tablespoons molasses, *Grandma's®***

1. Preheat oven to 400°F.

2. In a large pot, cook bacon over medium heat until slightly cooked but not crisp. With a slotted spoon, remove bacon to small bowl; set aside. Reserve bacon drippings in pot.

3. Cook onion in bacon drippings until soft. Stir in cooked bacon, baked beans, beer, ketchup, mustard, and molasses. Bring to a boil; reduce heat. Simmer for 10 minutes. Carefully transfer with a ladle to a 2-quart casserole dish. Place casserole on a foil-lined baking sheet.

4. Bake for 45 to 60 minutes or until beans reach desired thickness.

Scalloped and Mashed Potato Gratin

Prep 20 minutes **Bake** 35 minutes **Makes** 6 servings

- **Nonstick cooking spray, *Pam*®**
- 1 **bag (24-ounce) frozen cut red potatoes, *Ore-Ida*® *Steam n' Mash*®**
- ⅓ **cup evaporated milk, *Carnation*®**
- 1 **tablespoon onion soup mix, *Lipton*®**
- 3 **tablespoons butter**
- 1½ **cups shredded Colby and Monterey Jack cheese blend, *Sargento*®**
- ½ **cup frozen chopped onions, *Ore-Ida*®**
- ¼ **cup real bacon pieces, *Hormel*®**
- 1 **cup heavy cream**
- **Dash ground nutmeg, *McCormick*®**
- **Salt and ground black pepper**
- ¼ **cup bread crumbs, *Progresso*®**
- ½ **teaspoon paprika, *McCormick*®**

1. Preheat oven to 350°F. Lightly spray a 1½-quart baking dish with nonstick spray; set aside.

2. Microwave potatoes according to package directions. In a bowl, mash half the potatoes with the milk, soup mix, and 1 tablespoon of the butter. Spread mashed potatoes evenly into prepared baking dish. Sprinkle ½ cup of the cheese, half the onions, and half the bacon on the mashed potatoes. Add half the remaining unmashed potatoes to the dish in an even layer. Repeat layering cheese, onions, and bacon. Top with remaining unmashed potatoes.

3. In a small saucepan, heat the cream, nutmeg, and salt and pepper to taste over medium heat to just under a boil; pour over potatoes. Sprinkle remaining ½ cup of cheese on top. In a small bowl, stir together bread crumbs and paprika. Melt the remaining 2 tablespoons butter; stir into the bread crumbs. Sprinkle crumbs over the top of casserole.

4. Bake for 35 to 45 minutes or until bubbling and browned.

Creamy Ham Tart

Prep 15 minutes **Bake** 20 minutes + 25 minutes **Broil** 3 minutes **Cool** 10 minutes **Makes** 8 servings

- 1 sheet frozen puff pastry, thawed, *Pepperidge Farm®*
- 1 cup canned white sauce, *Aunt Penny's®*
- 1 cup diced ham, *John Morrell®*
- ½ cup shredded sharp cheddar cheese, *Sargento®*
- ¼ teaspoon nutmeg, *McCormick®*
- Salt and ground black pepper
- 1¼ cups grated Gruyère cheese

1. Preheat oven to 400°F.

2. Unroll puff pastry sheet and fold 2 inches from each corner into center of sheet. Roll sheet into a 10-inch circle with a rolling pin. Press puff pastry into broilerproof 9-inch tart pan. Press a piece of foil into bottom and up sides of puff pastry. Fill tart pan with pie weights or dried beans.

3. Bake for 15 to 18 minutes. Remove from oven and remove pie weights and foil. (Gently press down center of pastry if it puffs after removing weights.) Return to oven and bake for 5 to 8 minutes more or until golden. Remove and cool completely.

4. Reduce oven temperature to 350°F.

5. In a large bowl, stir together white sauce, ham, cheddar cheese, and nutmeg until well mixed. Season to taste with salt and pepper. Fill cooled crust with ham mixture. Sprinkle Gruyère cheese over top.

6. Bake for 25 to 30 minutes or until heated through. Remove from oven.

7. Preheat broiler. Cover edge of tart with foil. Broil tart 6 inches from heat for 3 to 5 minutes or until cheese is brown and bubbling. Remove and cool for 10 minutes. Slice and serve warm.

Southwest Baked Grits

Prep 10 minutes **Bake** 35 minutes **Makes** 8 servings

- **Nonstick cooking spray, *Pam*®**
- 2 **tubes (16 ounces each) Southern-style grits, *San Gennaro*®**
- 3 **tablespoons heavy cream**
- 1 **can (10-ounce) seasoned diced tomatoes and green chiles, drained, *Ro-Tel*®**
- 1 **can (4-ounce) diced green chiles, *Ortega*®**
- ¾ **cup Mexicorn, *Green Giant*®**
- 1½ **cups shredded 4-cheese Mexican cheese blend, *Sargento*®**
- **Salt and ground black pepper**

1. Preheat oven to 350°F. Spray a 2½-quart casserole dish with cooking spray; set aside.

2. In a large bowl, crumble grits, breaking up any whole pieces. Stir in cream, tomatoes, green chiles, Mexicorn, and 1 cup of the cheese. Season to taste with salt and pepper. Pour into prepared casserole dish. Top with remaining ½ cup cheese.

3. Bake for 35 to 40 minutes or until heated through. Serve warm.

Sesame Green Beans

Start to Finish 15 minutes **Makes** 4 servings

- 2 **teaspoons toasted sesame oil**
- 2 **teaspoons canola oil**
- 1 **box (10-ounce) frozen green beans, thawed and drained,** ***Green Giant®***
- 1 **tablespoon soy sauce,** ***Kikkoman®***
- 1 **tablespoon sesame seeds, toasted,** ***McCormick®***

1. In a large heavy skillet, heat sesame oil and canola oil over medium-high heat. Stir in the beans. Cook about 10 minutes or until the beans are slightly browned. Stir in soy sauce.

2. Transfer to a serving dish and top with toasted sesame seeds.

Mushroom and Pine Nut Risotto

Start to Finish 30 minutes  **Makes** 6 servings

- 1½ **cups white wine**
- 2 **cups vegetable broth,** ***Swanson®***
- 1 **cup milk**
- 2 **boxes (5.5 ounces each) garden vegetable risotto mix,** ***Buitoni®***
- 2 **jars (4.5 ounces each) sliced mushrooms, drained,** ***Green Giant®***
- ½ **cup pine nuts, toasted**
- ½ **cup grated Parmesan cheese,** ***DiGiorno®***
- 2 **tablespoons butter**
- **Grated Parmesan cheese**

1. In medium saucepan, combine wine, vegetable broth, and milk. Bring to a boil over high heat. Stir in risotto mix with seasoning packets and mushrooms. Reduce heat. Simmer, uncovered, for 20 to 24 minutes, stirring frequently. Remove from heat. Stir in pine nuts, Parmesan cheese, and butter. Top with additional Parmesan cheese. Serve immediately.

Pasta

Studies suggest that eating carbohydrates improves your mood. It's no wonder, then, that the world over, one of the most comforting foods is a big plate of noodles. After a few toothsome bites of perfectly cooked pasta—whether it's tossed with sauce or baked into a bubbly and creamy casserole—you can't help feeling better.

Grill Mates
TERIYAKI
MARINADE
FLAVOR
You Can See!

Chicken and Mushroom Baked Ziti

Prep 20 minutes **Bake** 15 minutes **Makes** 6 servings

- Nonstick cooking spray, *Pam®*
- 1 package (16-ounce) ziti pasta, *Ronzoni®*
- 3 tablespoons butter
- 1 package (8-ounce) sliced mushrooms
- ¾ cup frozen chopped onions, *Ore-Ida®*
- 1¼ cups half-and-half or light cream
- 1 packet (1.25-ounce) creamy garlic Alfredo sauce mix, *McCormick®*
- 2 tablespoons dry sherry, *Christian Brothers®*
- 1 can (10.75-ounce) condensed cream of mushroom soup, *Campbell's®*
- 2 packages (6 ounces each) grilled chicken breast strips, cut into bite-size strips, *Foster Farms®*
- 2 cups shredded mozzarella cheese, *Sargento®*
- Salt and ground black pepper
- ¼ cup grated Parmesan cheese, *DiGiorno®*

1. Preheat oven to 375°F. Spray a 9×13-inch baking pan with cooking spray; set aside.

2. In a large pot of boiling salted water, cook ziti according to package directions. Drain and set aside.

3. In a large skillet, heat butter over medium heat. Add mushrooms and onions; cook and stir for 5 to 7 minutes. Stir in half-and-half, sauce mix, and sherry. Bring to a boil; reduce heat. Stir in mushroom soup. Simmer for 3 to 5 minutes; remove from heat. Stir in cooked pasta, chicken, and 1 cup of the mozzarella until well mixed. Season to taste with salt and pepper. Transfer to prepared baking pan and top with the remaining 1 cup mozzarella and the Parmesan cheese.

4. Bake for 15 to 20 minutes or until cheese is melted. Serve hot.

Cajun Pasta Bake

Prep 20 minutes **Bake** 30 minutes **Makes** 6 servings

- **Nonstick cooking spray, *Pam*®**
- 1 **box (16-ounce) penne pasta, *Barilla*®**
- 1½ **cups chopped leftover meat (chicken, turkey, pork, or seafood)**
- 1 **tablespoon Cajun seasoning, *McCormick® Gourmet Collection***
- 1 **jar (16-ounce) Alfredo sauce with garlic, *Classico*®**
- 1 **can (14.5-ounce) diced tomatoes with green bell pepper and onion, drained, *S&W*®**
- ¾ **cup milk**
- ½ **cup grated Parmesan cheese, *DiGiorno*®**
- ½ **cup seasoned bread crumbs, *Progresso*®**
- 1 **tablespoon extra virgin olive oil**

1. Preheat oven to 350°F. Lightly spray a 3-quart casserole with cooking spray; set aside. In a large pot of boiling salted water, cook pasta according to package directions; drain.

2. In a large bowl, toss meat with 1½ teaspoons of the Cajun seasoning. Stir in Alfredo sauce, tomatoes, milk, Parmesan cheese, and remaining Cajun seasoning until well mixed. Add cooked pasta and stir to coat. Transfer to prepared casserole. In a small bowl, stir together bread crumbs and olive oil; sprinkle over casserole.

3. Bake for 30 to 40 minutes or until golden and bubbling around the edges. Serve hot.

Chicken Cheesy Mac

Prep 20 minutes **Bake** 20 minutes **Makes** 4 servings

- **1 package (12.6-ounce) Old World Italian Macaroni & Cheese Dinner with Parmesan & Romano Cheese Sauce, *Kraft® Homestyle Deluxe***
- **4 ounces cream cheese, softened, *Philadelphia®***
- **½ cup milk**
- **½ teaspoon garlic salt, *McCormick®***
- **¼ teaspoon ground black pepper**
- **2 cups frozen sliced carrots, *Birds Eye®***
- **1½ cups diced rotisserie chicken**
- **¼ cup plain bread crumbs, *Progresso®***
- **¼ cup grated Parmesan cheese, *Kraft®***
- **2 tablespoons butter, melted**

1. Preheat oven to 375°F. Remove bread crumb topping from Macaroni & Cheese Dinner; save for another use.

2. In a large saucepan, bring 6 cups of water to a boil. Stir in macaroni and cook for 7 minutes, stirring occasionally. Drain.

3. In a medium microwave-safe bowl, combine contents of cheese sauce pouch, cream cheese, milk, garlic salt, and pepper. Microwave on high for 1½ to 2 minutes or until sauce is smooth, stirring every 20 seconds.

4. In a large mixing bowl, combine macaroni, carrots, and chicken. Fold in sauce and stir until well mixed. Transfer to a 2-quart casserole dish.

5. In a small bowl, stir together bread crumbs, Parmesan, and melted butter; sprinkle on casserole. Bake for 20 to 25 minutes or until golden and bubbling.

Chicken Fettuccine

Start to Finish 25 minutes **Makes** 4 servings

- 1 **box (16-ounce) fettuccine pasta, *Barilla*®**
- 1 **tablespoon extra virgin olive oil**
- 1 **tablespoon bottled garlic puree, *Gourmet Garden*®**
- 2 **cans (15 ounces each) fire-roasted tomatoes with garlic, *Hunt's*®**
- 2 **cups shredded rotisserie chicken**
- ½ **cup sliced black olives, *Early California*®**
- ½ **cup sliced pimiento-stuffed green olives, *Early California*®**
- 1 **teaspoon Italian seasoning, *McCormick*®**
- 10 **fresh basil leaves, cut into thin strips**
- **Grated Parmesan cheese, *DiGiorno*®**

1. In a large pot of salted boiling water, cook pasta according to package directions. Drain, reserving ¾ cup pasta water.

2. While pasta cooks, in a large skillet, heat oil. Add garlic; cook and stir for 1 minute. Add tomatoes, chicken, olives, and Italian seasoning. Stir in ½ to ¾ cup pasta water for desired sauciness. Heat through. Stir in basil. Serve sauce over hot fettuccine and sprinkle each serving with Parmesan cheese.

Little Ears and Florets

Prep 20 minutes **Bake** 25 minutes **Makes** 6 servings

- 1 box (16-ounce) orecchiette pasta, *De Cecco®*
- 2 cups chopped leftover meat (chicken, turkey, pork, or seafood)
- 1 jar (16-ounce) Alfredo sauce with four cheeses, *Classico®*
- 1 bag (16-ounce) frozen broccoli and cauliflower, thawed, *Birds Eye®*
- 1 cup milk
- 3 cups shredded mozzarella cheese, *Sargento®*
- Salt and ground black pepper
- ¼ cup grated Parmesan cheese, *DiGiorno®*
- ¼ cup seasoned bread crumbs, *Progresso®*
- 2 tablespoons extra virgin olive oil

1. Preheat oven to 400°F. Lightly spray a 9×13-inch baking dish with cooking spray; set aside.

2. In a large pot of boiling salted water, cook pasta according to package directions; drain and return pasta to pot. Stir in chopped meat, Alfredo sauce, thawed vegetables, and milk. Stir in mozzarella until well mixed; season to taste with salt and pepper.

3. Transfer pasta mixture to prepared baking dish. In a small bowl, stir together Parmesan, bread crumbs, and olive oil; sprinkle over pasta. Bake for 25 to 30 minutes or until golden and bubbling. Serve hot.

Note: In Italian, orecchio means "ear." Orecchiette pasta resembles "little ears."

Butternut-Ricotta Pasta Bake

Prep 20 minutes **Bake** 20 minutes **Makes** 6 servings

- **Nonstick cooking spray, *Pam*®**
- 1 **package (16-ounce) fettuccine pasta, *Barilla*®**
- ¼ **cup butter**
- 2 **bags (8 ounces each) butternut squash, cut into ½-inch pieces, *Earth Exotic*®**
- 1¼ **cups chicken broth, *Swanson*®**
- ½ **cup milk**
- 1 **packet (1.6-ounce) garlic and herb sauce mix, *Knorr*®**
- 4 **ounces cream cheese, softened, *Philadelphia*®**
- 1 **cup ricotta cheese, *Precious*®**
- 2 **teaspoons sage leaves, *McCormick*® *Gourmet Collection***
- 1 **cup shredded 3-cheese blend, *DiGiorno*®**
- **Chopped fresh flat-leaf parsley (optional)**

1. Preheat oven to 350°F. Spray a 2½-quart casserole dish with cooking spray; set aside.

2. In a large pot of boiling salted water, cook pasta for 1 minute less than package directions. Drain and set aside.

3. In a large skillet, melt butter over medium heat. Add butternut squash; cook and stir about 4 minutes or until lightly caramelized. Stir in chicken broth, milk, and sauce mix. Bring to a boil, stirring occasionally. Reduce heat and simmer for 2 minutes. Remove from heat.

4. Add cooked pasta to skillet; stir until pasta is well coated. Transfer pasta-squash mixture to prepared casserole dish.

5. In a medium bowl, stir together cream cheese, ricotta cheese, and sage. Drop spoonfuls of ricotta mixture over pasta. Sprinkle shredded cheese over top. Tightly cover baking dish with foil.

6. Bake for 15 minutes or until ricotta mixture is heated through and cheese is melted. Uncover and bake 5 more minutes or until cheese is golden brown. Top with chopped parsley (optional).

Pasta Portobello

Prep 25 minutes **Bake** 45 minutes **Makes** 6 servings

- **Nonstick cooking spray, *Pam*®**
- 1 **box (16-ounce) rigatoni pasta, *Barilla*®**
- 3 **large portobello mushrooms**
- 2 **tablespoons extra virgin olive oil**
- 1 **cup frozen chopped onions, *Ore-Ida*®**
- 1 **tablespoon bottled garlic puree, *Gourmet Garden*®**
- 1 **jar (26-ounce) marinara sauce with red wine, *Newman's Own*®**
- 1½ **cups chopped leftover meat (chicken, turkey, pork, ham, sausage, or beef)**
- ¼ **teaspoon red pepper flakes, *McCormick*®**
- 3 **cups shredded mozzarella cheese, *Sargento*®**
- 1 **container (15-ounce) low-fat ricotta cheese, *Precious*®**

1. Preheat oven to 400°F. Lightly spray a 9x13-inch baking dish with cooking spray; set aside.

2. In a large pot of boiling salted water, cook pasta according to package directions; drain and return to pot.

3. While pasta cooks, remove stems and gills from mushrooms, then roughly chop. In a large skillet, heat oil over medium-high heat. Add chopped mushrooms, onions, and garlic; cook and stir for 5 to 7 minutes or until mushrooms are soft. Stir in marinara sauce, chopped meat, and red pepper flakes. Bring to a boil. Remove from heat and stir into cooked pasta along with 2 cups of the mozzarella. Drop ricotta into the pot by spoonfuls and gently fold through.

4. Transfer to prepared baking dish and top with remaining mozzarella. Cover dish loosely with aluminum foil. Bake for 35 minutes. Remove foil and continue baking about 10 minutes more or until cheese is golden and bubbling. Serve hot.

Penne Pasta with Sausage

Start to Finish 25 minutes **Makes** 4 servings

- 1 **box (16-ounce) penne pasta, *Barilla*®**
- 2 **tablespoons extra virgin olive oil**
- 1 **small onion, diced**
- 1 **tablespoon Italian seasoning, *McCormick*®**
- 2 **teaspoons bottled chopped garlic, *Gourmet Garden*®**
- ¼ **teaspoon crushed red pepper flakes (optional), *McCormick*®**
- 4 **hot Italian-style pork sausages, cooked and cut into ½-inch slices**
- 1 **can (28-ounce) crushed tomatoes, *Hunt's*®**
- ¼ **cup heavy cream**
- **Kosher salt and ground black pepper**
- 2 **tablespoons chopped fresh basil**

1. In a large pot of boiling salted water, cook pasta according to package directions. Drain.

2. In a large deep skillet, heat olive oil over medium-high heat. Add onion, Italian seasoning mix, garlic, and red pepper flakes (if using); cook for 3 to 4 minutes or until onions are soft and fragrant, stirring frequently. Add sausages and cook for 1 minute. Stir in tomatoes. Cover and simmer for 10 minutes. Stir in cream. Season to taste with salt and pepper. Stir pasta into sauce in skillet. Sprinkle with fresh basil.

Cheesy Garlic Bread

Prep 10 minutes **Bake** 10 minutes **Makes** 4 servings

- 1 **loaf store-bought garlic bread**
- 1 **cup shredded mozzarella cheese, *Kraft*®**
- ½ **teaspoon Italian seasoning, *McCormick*®**

1. Preheat oven to 400°F.

2. Sprinkle cheese and Italian seasoning on garlic bread. Place on foil-lined baking sheet. Bake for 10 to 12 minutes or until the cheese is melted and bread is heated through. Slice and serve.

Ravioli Lasagna

5-quart slow cooker **Prep** 15 minutes **Cook** 4 hours (low) **Makes** 4 servings

Nonstick cooking spray, *Pam®*

- 1 **pound ground hot Italian sausage, *Johnsonville®***
- 1 **tablespoon bottled garlic puree, *Gourmet Garden®***
- 1 **jar (26-ounce) marinara sauce with mushrooms, *Newman's Own®***
- 1 **bag (26-ounce) frozen large ravioli, *Celentano®***
- 2 **cups shredded 6-cheese Italian cheese blend, *Sargento®***

1. Spray the inside of the slow cooker with cooking spray.

2. In a large skillet, brown sausage with garlic over medium heat. Spread 1 cup of marinara in the bottom of the slow cooker. Place one-third of ravioli in an even layer in slow cooker. Top with half the sausage, ¾ cup of cheese, and ½ cup sauce. Repeat layers and top with remaining third of ravioli. Spread remaining sauce over top and sprinkle with remaining cheese. Cover and cook on low for 4 hours.

Grilled Veggies Rigatoni

Start to Finish 25 minutes **Makes** 4 servings

- **1 box (16-ounce) rigatoni pasta, *Barilla*®**
- **3 tablespoons extra virgin olive oil**
- **2 small Italian eggplants, sliced in ½-inch-thick disks**
- **1 zucchini, sliced in half lengthwise**
- **1 small onion, sliced**
- **1 red bell pepper**
- **2 tablespoons extra virgin olive oil**
- **1 tablespoon bottled chopped garlic, *Gourmet Garden*®**
- **Red pepper flakes, *McCormick*®**
- **Salt and ground black pepper**

1. Set up grill for direct cooking over medium-high heat. Or preheat a grill pan over medium-high heat.

2. In a large pot of boiling salted water, cook pasta according to package directions. Drain pasta and drizzle with about 1 teaspoon of the olive oil to prevent pasta from sticking together.

3. Lightly brush eggplant, zucchini, onion, and bell pepper with the remaining olive oil. Place vegetables on grill or in grill pan and grill for 3 minutes per side. Remove vegetables; cool for 5 minutes. Slice vegetables into bite-size pieces.

4. In the pot used to cook the pasta, heat the 2 tablespoons olive oil over medium heat. Add garlic and red pepper flakes to taste; cook and stir for 1 minute. Add chopped vegetables and pasta to pot and toss all together. Season to taste with salt and pepper. Serve immediately.

Spaghetti with Meatballs

Prep 20 minutes **Bake** 12 minutes **Cook** 25 minutes **Makes** 4 servings

MEATBALLS

Nonstick cooking spray, *Pam*®
- **2 slices white bread, cut into cubes**
- **¼ cup milk**
- **1 egg**
- **½ medium onion, diced**
- **1 tablespoon Italian seasoning, *McCormick*®**
- **2 teaspoons bottled chopped garlic, *Gourmet Garden*®**
- **½ teaspoon salt**
- **¼ teaspoon ground black pepper, *McCormick*®**
- **1 pound lean ground beef**
- **2 sticks mozzarella string cheese, cut into small cubes**

SAUCE

- **2 tablespoons extra virgin olive oil**
- **½ medium onion, diced**
- **1 tablespoon bottled chopped garlic, *Gourmet Garden*®**
- **1 can (28-ounce) diced tomatoes, *Hunt's*®**
- **2 tablespoons chopped fresh basil**
- **2 tablespoons chopped fresh parsley**
- **Salt and ground black pepper**
- **1 box (16-ounce) spaghetti, *Barilla*®**

1. For the meatballs, preheat oven to 400°F. Spray a baking sheet with cooking spray; set aside.

2. In a large bowl, combine bread and milk. Let stand about 5 minutes or until bread absorbs the milk. Stir in egg, onion, Italian seasoning, garlic, salt, and pepper. Add ground beef and mix well. For each meatball, press about 3 tablespoons of the meat mixture into a patty. Place a mozzarella cube on the center of the patty; bring up the sides around the cheese and roll into a ball. Place on prepared baking sheet. Repeat process with remaining meat and cheese. Bake meatballs for 12 minutes.

3. While the meatballs bake, prepare the sauce. In a medium pot, heat olive oil over medium heat. Add onion and garlic and cook for 3 minutes. Add tomatoes, basil, parsley, and salt and pepper to taste. Simmer for 10 minutes. Gently stir in meatballs and any pan drippings from baking sheet.

4. Meanwhile, in a large pot of boiling salted water, cook spaghetti according to package directions; drain. Serve sauce and meatballs over spaghetti.

Note: To make Spaghetti and Meatball Calzones (see recipe, page 128), double the ingredients in this recipe for both the meatballs and sauce.

Spaghetti and Meatball Calzones

Prep 15 minutes **Bake** 35 minutes **Makes** 4 servings

- 1 **package (16-ounce) refrigerated pizza dough, *Pillsbury*®**
- **Leftover spaghetti and meatballs, meatballs chopped (see recipe, page 126)**
- ½ **cup leftover spaghetti sauce (see recipe, page 126)**
- ¼ **cup shredded mozzarella cheese, *Kraft*®**
- **Tomato sauce (optional)**

1. Preheat oven to 400°F. Line a baking sheet with parchment paper; set aside.

2. Divide the dough into four equal portions. On a floured work surface, roll each piece of dough with a rolling pin into a 6- to 8-inch round.

3. Place one-fourth of the leftover spaghetti and meatballs in the center of one of the dough rounds. Top with 1 tablespoon of sauce and sprinkle with 1 tablespoon of cheese. Brush the edges of the dough with water. Fold the dough over to make a half circle and crimp the edge with a fork. Place on prepared baking sheet. Repeat with remaining dough and filling.

4. Bake about 35 minutes or until golden. Serve hot with a side of tomato sauce (optional).

Breakfast for Dinner?

Most mornings you likely have little time for much more than a bowl of cereal or a granola bar. But when you can move leisurely, surprise your family with one of these recipes. This collection of hearty egg dishes, bakery-quality pastries, and warm-from-the-oven coffee cakes will start (or end) your day in a most satisfying way.

Eggs Benedict
with Microwave Hollandaise

Start to Finish 35 minutes **Makes** 6 servings

- **1 box (6-ounce) frozen petite French-style croissants, *Sara Lee*®**

HOLLANDAISE SAUCE

- **3 tablespoons butter**
- **2 tablespoons all-purpose flour**
- **1 cup hot water**
- **2 tablespoons frozen lemon juice, thawed, *Minute Maid*®**
- **2 egg yolks**
- **Pinch cayenne pepper, *McCormick*®**
- **Salt and ground black pepper**

EGGS BENEDICT

- **6 eggs, beaten**
- **6 slices prosciutto, thinly sliced**
- **Fresh tarragon leaves (optional)**

1. Preheat oven to 325°F. Horizontally slice frozen croissants, leaving croissants intact. Place on ungreased baking sheet. Bake for 7 to 9 minutes while preparing hollandaise sauce.

2. For hollandaise sauce, place butter in a medium microwave-safe bowl. Microwave, uncovered, on high about 20 seconds to melt butter. Stir in flour. Slowly stir in hot water and lemon juice. Microwave on high for 1½ to 2 minutes or until sauce thickens, stirring twice. Quickly whisk in egg yolks. Microwave on medium for 1½ to 2 minutes or until sauce thickens. Remove and stir in cayenne. Season to taste with salt and pepper; cover to keep warm.

3. For eggs, fill a medium skillet halfway with water. Bring water to a simmer over medium heat (do not boil). Working with one egg at a time, crack egg into a small bowl and slide into simmering water. Simmer eggs for 3 to 5 minutes or until whites are cooked and yolk is still soft. With a slotted spoon, transfer eggs to a plate.*

4. Separate croissant halves and place together forming a circle, cut sides up. Top with a slice of prosciutto and poached egg. Spoon hollandaise sauce over top of egg. Garnish with tarragon leaves (optional).

***Note:** Eggs can be precooked and refrigerated to this point. At serving time, reheat by sliding egg into simmering water for 1 minute.

Bacon-Tomato Quiche

Prep 10 minutes **Bake** 25 minutes + 30 minutes **Cool/Stand** 20 minutes **Makes** 6 servings

MASHED POTATO CRUST

- **Nonstick cooking spray, *Pam*®**
- 1 **bag (24-ounce) frozen cut russet potatoes, *Ore-Ida*® *Steam n' Mash*®**
- ½ **cup evaporated milk, *Carnation*®**
- ¼ **cup shredded Parmesan cheese, *DiGiorno*®**
- 1 **egg, lightly beaten**

TOMATO AND BACON FILLING

- 2 **cups shredded Monterey Jack cheese, *Sargento*®**
- 1 **can (15-ounce) diced tomatoes with garlic and basil, well drained, *Hunt's*®**
- ⅓ **cup real crumbled bacon, *Hormel*®**
- 3 **eggs**
- 1 **cup half-and-half**
- ½ **teaspoon salt**
- ¼ **teaspoon ground black pepper**
- ¼ **teaspoon dried thyme, *McCormick*®**

1. Preheat oven to 350°F. Lightly spray a 9-inch square tart pan or round baking dish with cooking spray; set aside.

2. For mashed potato crust, microwave potatoes according to package directions. In a medium bowl, mash cooked potatoes with milk. Stir in Parmesan and egg until well mixed. Press into bottom and up the sides of tart pan or baking dish and spray lightly with cooking spray.

3. Bake for 25 to 30 minutes or until lightly golden. Remove mashed potato crust from oven and cool for 10 to 15 minutes.

4. For tomato and bacon filling, sprinkle half the Monterey Jack cheese in the crust. Layer tomatoes, bacon, and remaining cheese. In a small bowl, beat together eggs, half-and-half, salt, pepper, and thyme; pour over filling.

5. Bake for 30 to 40 minutes or until a knife inserted 1 inch off-center comes away clean. Let stand 10 minutes before slicing.

Potato and Bacon Quiche

Prep 25 minutes **Bake** 50 minutes **Cool** 30 minutes **Makes** 10 servings

- **1** **refrigerated piecrust, *Pillsbury*®**
- **2¼** **cups refrigerated hash browns, *Reser's*®**
- **½** **cup crumbled cooked bacon, *Hormel*®**
- **5** **tablespoons crumbled blue cheese, *Sargento*®**
- **2** **teaspoons salt-free garlic and herb seasoning, *McCormick*®**
- **¼** **teaspoon paprika, *McCormick*®**
- **½** **cup egg substitute, *Egg Beaters*®**
- **½** **cup heavy cream**
- **⅓** **cup milk**

1. Preheat oven to 350°F.

2. On a lightly floured surface, unroll piecrust; fold two sides of circle toward center. Roll into a 12×8-inch rectangle with a rolling pin and press into tart pan. Press a piece of foil into bottom and up sides of crust. Fill tart pan with baking beans.

3. Bake tart crust for 10 to 15 minutes. Remove from oven; remove baking beans and foil. Return to oven and bake for 5 to 8 minutes more or until golden brown. Cool completely, about 20 minutes.

4. In a large bowl, stir together hash browns, bacon, 2 tablespoons of the blue cheese, garlic and herb seasoning, and paprika until well mixed. Spoon potato mixture into cooled crust. In a medium bowl, whisk together egg substitute, cream, and milk until well combined. Pour over potato mixture in pan. Sprinkle remaining 3 tablespoons blue cheese over top.

5. Bake for 35 to 40 minutes or until center is set. Remove from oven and cool for 10 minutes. Cut into squares and serve warm or at room temperature.

Ham and Cheese Frittata

Prep 10 minutes **Bake** 35 minutes **Makes** 6 servings

- **Nonstick cooking spray, *Pam*®**
- 1 **cup precooked rosemary potatoes, *Reser's*®**
- 1 **cup cubed ham, *Farmland*®**
- 1 **cup shredded Colby and Monterey Jack cheese blend, *Kraft*®**
- 4 **eggs**
- 1½ **cups milk**
- ½ **teaspoon salt**
- ¼ **teaspoon ground black pepper**
- 1 **teaspoon salt-free all-purpose seasoning, *McCormick*®**

1. Preheat oven to 400°F. Spray a 9-inch pie plate with cooking spray. Arrange potatoes, ham, and cheese in bottom of pie plate; set aside.

2. In a medium bowl, stir together eggs, milk, salt, pepper, and seasoning. Pour into pie plate.

3. Bake for 35 to 40 minutes or until eggs set. Remove from oven and cool for 5 minutes. Serve warm or at room temperature.

Note: This can be made in advance, refrigerated, and reheated in a microwave.

Breakfast Pancake Roll

Prep 10 minuets **Bake** 8 minutes **Makes** 8 servings

- 1½ cups pancake mix, *Aunt Jemima*®
- 1¼ cups milk
- 2 eggs
- 2 teaspoons sugar
- 1½ cups egg substitute, *Egg Beaters*®
- ½ cup crumbled cooked bacon, *Hormel*®
- ½ cup shredded mild cheddar cheese, *Sargento*®
- Salt and ground black pepper
- Maple syrup

1. Preheat oven to 450°F. Line a 10×15-inch jelly-roll pan with parchment paper and spray with cooking spray; set aside.

2. Stir together pancake mix, milk, eggs, and sugar. Pour into jelly-roll pan.

3. Bake for 8 to 10 minutes or until tester comes out clean. Cool for 5 minutes. Lift one edge of parchment paper from short side and roll carefully. Place a clean kitchen towel on top of roll to keep it from unrolling. Cool completely.

4. Spray a large skillet with cooking spray and heat over medium heat. Pour in egg substitute. Cook without stirring until edges and bottom begin to set. Add bacon and flip cooked part of egg. Continue to cook eggs until set. Sprinkle cheese over top and remove from heat. Season with salt and pepper.

5. Unroll cake. Arrange eggs on top, leaving a ¾-inch border on each of the long sides and the farthest short side. Lift same edge of parchment paper as before and reroll cake, peeling parchment paper away from cake as you roll. Transfer to a serving plate, seam side down. Slice and serve with maple syrup.

Swedish Puffs

Prep 10 minutes **Rise** 1½ hours **Bake** 12 minutes **Makes** 12 servings

- 12 frozen Parker House rolls
- 1 tablespoon + 1 teaspoon cinnamon-sugar, *McCormick*®
- 1 teaspoon ground cardamom, *McCormick*®
- ½ teaspoon ground nutmeg, *McCormick*®
- 3 tablespoons butter, melted
- 1½ cups whipped topping, thawed, *Cool Whip*®
- ¾ cup almond cake and pastry filling, *Solo*®
- Sifted powdered sugar, *C&H*®

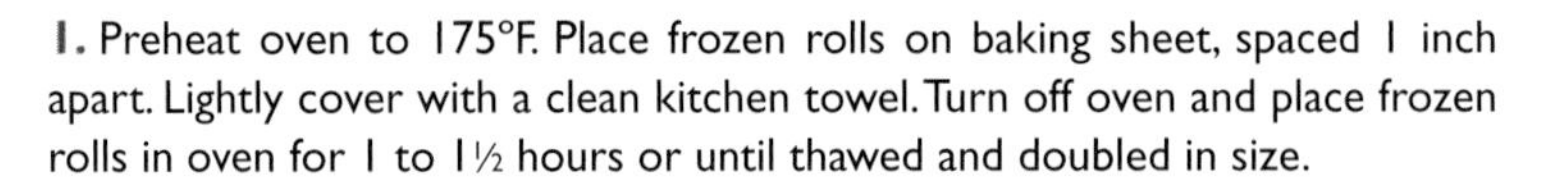

1. Preheat oven to 175°F. Place frozen rolls on baking sheet, spaced 1 inch apart. Lightly cover with a clean kitchen towel. Turn off oven and place frozen rolls in oven for 1 to 1½ hours or until thawed and doubled in size.

2. In a shallow bowl, combine cinnamon-sugar, cardamom, and nutmeg; set aside. Remove rolls from oven. Place one roll on a flat surface. Press center of roll with finger and fold dough in on itself. Form into a ball, then roll in spice mixture until well coated. Repeat with all rolls. Place on greased baking sheets, spaced 2 inches apart; cover with a towel and let rise for 30 minutes.

3. Preheat oven to 375°F. Brush melted butter on each roll with a pastry brush. Bake rolls for 12 to 14 minutes. Remove and cool completely.

4. For spiced cream, in a small bowl, stir together whipped topping and the remaining 1 tablespoon of spice mixture; cover and refrigerate until ready to use.

5. Cut off bun top. Remove half of bread from center of bun. Fill with 1 tablespoon almond filling and 2 tablespoons spiced cream. Replace top; dust with powdered sugar.

Strawberry-Stuffed French Toast

Start to Finish 25 minutes **Makes** 4 servings

- 1 package (8-ounce) cream cheese, softened, *Philadelphia*®
- 2 tablespoons strawberry preserves, *Smucker's*®
- 1 tablespoon shredded orange zest
- 4 eggs
- 1 cup half-and-half
- 2 tablespoons Grand Marnier or frozen orange juice concentrate, thawed
- 1½ teaspoons vanilla extract, *McCormick*®
- 8 slices Texas-toast-style bread
- Butter
- Strawberry syrup, *Smucker's*®
- Sliced fresh strawberries (optional)
- Powdered sugar (optional)

1. In a small mixing bowl, stir together softened cream cheese, strawberry preserves, and orange zest until smooth. Set aside.

2. In a bowl, whisk together the eggs, half-and-half, Grand Marnier, and vanilla extract. Pour into a shallow bowl or pie plate. Set aside.

3. With a paring knife, slice a pocket into the side of each bread slice (do not cut all the way through the bread). Fill bread slices with a heaping spoonful of cream cheese mixture.

4. In a skillet, melt some butter over medium heat. Dip filled bread in egg mixture and brown for 1 to 2 minutes per side in hot butter. Serve hot with strawberry syrup, fresh sliced strawberries, and powdered sugar (optional).

Chai Coffee Cake

Prep 10 minutes **Bake** 40 minutes **Makes** 9 servings

- **Nonstick cooking spray, *Pam®***
- **1 box (14.5-ounce) gingerbread cake and cookie mix, *Krusteaz®***
- **1 cup chai tea concentrate,* *Tazo®***
- **1 egg**
- **2 teaspoons chai spice, *McCormick®***
- **1 cup baking mix, *Bisquick®***
- **⅓ cup packed brown sugar, *C&H®***
- **1 teaspoon ground cinnamon, *McCormick®***
- **6 tablespoons butter, chilled, cut into tiny pieces**

1. Preheat oven to 350°F. Spray an 8×8-inch square cake pan with cooking spray; set aside.

2. In a large bowl, stir together cake and cookie mix, tea concentrate, egg, and 1 teaspoon of the chai spice until mixed. Pour into prepared pan.

3. In a medium bowl, stir together baking mix, brown sugar, remaining 1 teaspoon chai spice, and cinnamon. Work in butter pieces with hands until mixture is crumbly. Sprinkle over cake batter in pan.

4. Bake for 40 to 45 minutes or until a tester comes out clean. Cool completely. Cut into squares to serve.

***Note:** Look for this product in the tea section of a large supermarket.

Buttermilk Potato Cakes

Prep 15 minutes **Cook** 12 minutes **Makes** 4 servings

- **1 bag (22-ounce) frozen cut russet potatoes, *Ore-Ida® Steam n' Mash®***
- **¼ cup buttermilk**
- **2 tablespoons butter**
- **1 egg, lightly beaten**
- **2 tablespoons chopped fresh parsley**
- **1 teaspoon ground mustard powder, *McCormick®***
- **½ teaspoon garlic powder, *McCormick®***
- **All-purpose flour**
- **2 tablespoons extra virgin olive oil**
- **Kosher salt**
- **Crumbled cooked bacon, *Hormel®* (optional)**
- **Chopped fresh chives (optional)**

1. Cook potatoes according to package directions. In a bowl, mash potatoes with buttermilk and butter. Stir in egg, parsley, mustard, and garlic powder. Shape mixture into eight patties. Dredge patties in flour, shaking off excess.

2. In a large nonstick skillet, heat oil over medium-high heat. Fry half the patties in hot oil for 3 minutes or until nicely browned. Gently turn cakes over and cook 3 minutes more. Drain on paper towels. Repeat with remaining patties. Season with salt. Top with crumbled cooked bacon and chives (optional).

Almond Croissants

Prep 15 minutes **Bake** 12 minutes **Makes** 8 servings

- ½ **cup almond paste, *Odense*®**
- 3 **tablespoons spiced rum, *Captain Morgan*®**
- 2 **tablespoons packed brown sugar, *C&H*®**
- ¾ **teaspoon ground cinnamon, *McCormick*®**
- 1 **can (8-ounce) refrigerated crescent rolls, *Pillsbury*®**
- 1 **egg, lightly beaten with 1 teaspoon water**
- 3 **tablespoons sliced almonds, *Planters*®**
- 1 **cup French vanilla whipped topping, thawed, *Cool Whip*®**

1. Preheat oven to 375°F. In a small bowl, grate almond paste. Stir in rum, brown sugar, and cinnamon until well mixed; set aside.

2. Unroll a crescent roll to lie flat. Spread 1 tablespoon of almond mixture in the middle and roll to make croissant. Place on a baking sheet. Repeat with remaining ingredients to make eight croissants total. Using a pastry brush, brush beaten egg on each croissant. Sprinkle sliced almonds on top.

3. Bake for 12 to 15 minutes or until golden brown. Remove and cool completely. To serve, top with whipped topping.

Casseroles

Pulled bubbling from the oven, a casserole consoles a weary soul at the end of even the most difficult day. I love that casseroles are convenient—many of them are one-dish meals—and in every bite, you get a variety of complementary textures and a taste of all the wonderful flavors that have mingled with one another during cooking.

Cowboy Meat Loaf and Potato Casserole

Prep 15 minutes **Bake** 20 minutes + 15 minutes **Makes** 6 servings

- 1½ **pounds lean ground beef**
- ¾ **cup frozen chopped onions, thawed, *Ore-Ida*®**
- ⅓ **cup seasoned bread crumbs, *Progresso*®**
- 1 **egg, slightly beaten**
- ¼ **cup barbecue sauce, *Bulls-Eye*®**
- 1 **packet (1.25-ounce) taco seasoning, *McCormick*®**
- ½ **teaspoon salt**
- 1 **bag (24-ounce) frozen cut russet potatoes, *Ore-Ida*® *Steam n' Mash*®**
- ⅔ **cup evaporated milk, *Carnation*®**
- 1 **tablespoon butter**
- ½ **cup real crumbled bacon, *Hormel*®**
- ½ **cup french-fried onions, *French's*®**
- **Salt and ground black pepper**
- 1 **cup shredded 4-cheese Mexican cheese blend, *Sargento*®**

1. Preheat oven to 375°F.

2. In large bowl, combine ground beef, onions, bread crumbs, beaten egg, barbecue sauce, taco seasoning, and ½ teaspoon salt. Mix thoroughly, then gently press into the bottom of a 9-inch square baking pan. Bake for 20 to 25 minutes or until cooked through. Carefully pour off drippings.

3. Meanwhile, microwave potatoes according to package directions. In a medium bowl, mash cooked potatoes with milk and butter. Stir in bacon and fried onions. Season to taste with salt and pepper. Spread over meat loaf to the edges of the pan; sprinkle with cheese. Return to oven for 15 minutes. Slice and serve.

Reuben Casserole

Prep 25 minutes **Bake** 25 minutes **Makes** 6 servings

- 3 **slices dark rye bread, *Oroweat*®**
- **Nonstick cooking spray, *Pam*®**
- 1 **teaspoon garlic salt, *McCormick*®**
- 1 **package (12-ounce) wide egg noodles, *Manischewitz*®**
- 1¼ **cups milk**
- 1 **packet (1.6-ounce) garlic and herb sauce mix, *Knorr*®**
- 2 **tablespoons spicy brown mustard, *Gulden's*®**
- ½ **teaspoon caraway seeds, *McCormick® Gourmet Collection* (optional)**
- 3 **cups sauerkraut, drained, *Bubbies*®**
- 1½ **pounds deli corned beef, chopped**
- ¾ **cup Thousand Island salad dressing, *Ken's Steak House*®**
- ¾ **cup frozen chopped onions, *Ore-Ida*®**
- 2 **cups grated Swiss cheese**

1. Preheat oven to 400°F. Line a baking sheet with foil and set aside.

2. Cut rye bread into bite-size pieces. Spread pieces in an even layer on prepared baking sheet. Spray bread with cooking spray and sprinkle with garlic salt. Bake about 10 minutes or until dried. Remove and cool completely.

3. Reduce oven temperature to 375°F. Spray a 3-quart casserole dish with cooking spray and set aside.

4. In a large pot of boiling salted water, cook egg noodles about 8 minutes or until tender but not quite al dente. Drain and set aside.

5. In a large saucepan, combine milk, garlic and herb sauce mix, mustard, and caraway seeds (optional). Bring to a boil; reduce heat. Simmer for 1 minute. Remove from heat. Stir in sauerkraut, corned beef, salad dressing, onions, and 1 cup of the Swiss cheese until well mixed. Stir in noodles, stirring just until combined. Transfer to prepared casserole dish. Top with remaining 1 cup Swiss cheese. Crush rye bread pieces into fine crumbs and sprinkle over casserole. Cover with foil.

6. Bake for 20 minutes. Remove foil and bake about 5 to 10 minutes more or until heated through. Serve hot.

Pizza Casserole

Prep 20 minutes **Bake** 30 minutes **Makes** 8 servings

- **Nonstick cooking spray, *Pam*®**
- **1 package (16-ounce) mini penne pasta, *Barilla*®**
- **1 jar (26-ounce) pasta sauce, *Prego*®**
- **1 container (5-ounce) diced bell peppers, chopped, *Ready Pac*® *Tri Peppers***
- **1½ teaspoons Italian seasoning, *McCormick*®**
- **5 cups shredded mozzarella cheese, *Sargento*®**
- **1 jar (4.5-ounce) sliced mushrooms, drained, *Green Giant*®**
- **1 can (3.8-ounce) sliced black olives, drained, *Early California*®**
- **½ package (3.5-ounce) sliced pepperoni (25 slices), *Hormel*®**
- **⅓ cup grated Parmesan cheese, *DiGiorno*®**
- **1 roll (8-ounce) garlic breadsticks, *Pillsbury*®**

1. Preheat oven to 350°F. Spray a 9×13-inch baking dish with cooking spray; set aside.

2. In a large pot of boiling salted water, cook penne for 7 minutes or until tender but not quite al dente. Drain well. In a large bowl, stir together cooked penne, pasta sauce, chopped peppers, and Italian seasoning. Stir in 3 cups of the mozzarella cheese until well mixed. Transfer to prepared dish. Sprinkle 1 cup of the remaining mozzarella over top. Top with sliced mushrooms and olives. Sprinkle remaining 1 cup of mozzarella over top. Arrange pepperoni slices over mozzarella; sprinkle with Parmesan cheese.

3. Bake for 15 minutes. Remove breadstick dough from can and separate into individual strips. Fold each strip in half and twist. Remove casserole from oven and place twisted dough around edge of baking dish. Return to oven; bake for 15 to 18 minutes more or until breadsticks are golden brown. Serve hot.

Chicken and Dumplings Casserole

Prep 15 minutes **Bake** 35 minutes **Makes** 6 servings

- **Nonstick cooking spray, *Pam*®**
- **¼ cup butter**
- **1 cup carrot and celery sticks, finely chopped, *Ready Pac*® *Party Pac***
- **½ cup diced onions, *Ready Pac*®**
- **2 teaspoons bottled garlic blend, *Gourmet Garden*®**
- **1 teaspoon poultry seasoning, *McCormick*®**
- **2 jars (12 ounces each) chicken gravy, *Heinz*®**
- **1 store-bought rotisserie chicken, skin and bones removed, meat cut into bite-size pieces**
- **2¼ cups frozen petite peas, *C & W*®**
- **Salt and ground black pepper**
- **2 cups baking mix, *Bisquick*®**
- **⅔ cup buttermilk**
- **2 teaspoons finely chopped fresh flat-leaf parsley**

1. Preheat oven to 350°F. Spray a 9×13-inch baking dish with cooking spray and set aside.

2. In a large saucepan, heat butter over medium heat. Cook and stir chopped carrot and celery, onions, garlic, and poultry seasoning until tender. Stir in gravy. Bring to a boil. Stir in chicken and peas; season to taste with salt and pepper. Transfer to prepared baking dish and set aside.

3. For dumplings, in a medium bowl, stir together baking mix, buttermilk, and parsley until moistened. Drop by tablespoonfuls onto casserole.

4. Bake, uncovered, for 25 minutes. Cover with foil and bake about 10 minutes more or until dumplings are cooked through. Serve hot.

Casserole à la Grecque

Prep 25 minutes **Bake** 30 minutes **Makes** 6 servings

- **Nonstick cooking spray, *Pam*®**
- 1 **box (16 ounces) gemelli pasta, *Barilla*®**
- 2 **tablespoons extra virgin olive oil**
- ¾ **cup diced onions, *Ready Pac*®**
- 1 **pound ground lamb**
- 1 **tablespoon Greek seasoning, *McCormick*®**
- 2 **teaspoons bottled garlic blend, *Gourmet Garden*®**
- ½ **teaspoon ground cinnamon, *McCormick*®**
- 1 **can (10.5-ounce) white sauce, *Aunt Penny's*®**
- ¼ **cup half-and-half**
- ¼ **teaspoon ground nutmeg, *McCormick*®**
- 1 **can (15-ounce) diced tomatoes with basil and garlic, *Muir Glen*®**
- 1 **box (10-ounce) frozen chopped spinach, thawed and squeezed dry, *Birds Eye*®**
- **Salt and ground black pepper**
- 1 **cup grated Parmesan cheese, *DiGiorno*®**
- ¾ **cup crumbled feta cheese, *Kraft*®**

1. Preheat oven to 350°F. Spray a 9×13-inch baking dish with cooking spray and set aside.

2. In a large pot of boiling salted water, cook pasta for 12 minutes or until tender but not quite al dente. Drain and set aside. In a large skillet, heat oil over medium high heat. Cook and stir onions until tender. Add ground lamb, Greek seasoning, garlic, and cinnamon. Brown lamb, stirring frequently to break into small pieces. Remove from heat and set aside.

3. Place white sauce, half-and-half, and nutmeg in a large microwave-safe bowl. Microwave for 2 minutes or until heated through. Stir in tomatoes and spinach until well mixed. Season to taste with salt and pepper. Stir in cooked pasta.

4. Layer half of pasta mixture into prepared dish. Sprinkle with half the Parmesan cheese. Repeat layering with remaining ingredients. Sprinkle feta cheese over top.

5. Bake for 30 to 40 minutes or until heated through.

Chicken Cordon Bleu Casserole

Prep 15 minutes **Bake** 45 minutes **Makes** 4 servings

- **Nonstick cooking spray, *Pam*®**
- **1 cup converted white rice, *Uncle Ben's*®**
- **1 can (10.75-ounce) condensed cream of chicken soup, *Campbell's*®**
- **¾ cup chicken broth, *Swanson*®**
- **¼ cup white wine**
- **1½ teaspoons dried oregano, *McCormick*®**
- **2 tablespoons extra virgin olive oil**
- **½ cup frozen chopped onions, *Ore-Ida*®**
- **2 teaspoons bottled garlic blend, *Gourmet Garden*®**
- **1 pound boneless, skinless chicken breasts, cut into bite-size pieces**
- **Salt and ground black pepper**
- **½ pound ham steak, cubed**
- **1½ cups grated Swiss cheese**
- **½ box (5.5-ounce) seasoned coating mix for chicken, *Shake n' Bake*®**
- **2 tablespoons butter, melted**

1. Preheat oven to 375°F. Spray a 2½-quart casserole dish with cooking spray and set aside.

2. In a medium bowl, stir together rice, cream of chicken soup, chicken broth, white wine, and oregano until well mixed. Spoon into the prepared casserole dish and set aside.

3. In a large skillet, heat oil over medium-high heat. Add onions and garlic. Cook and stir until tender. Season chicken pieces with salt and pepper and add to skillet. Cook and stir just until cooked and lightly browned. Remove from heat and stir in ham. Spread over rice in casserole. Sprinkle Swiss cheese over the top.

4. In a small bowl, stir together coating mix and melted butter; sprinkle over cheese. Cover tightly with foil. Bake for 35 minutes. Remove foil and bake for another 10 minutes. Serve hot.

Chicken Chilaquiles

Prep 20 minutes **Bake** 10 minutes **Makes** 5 or 6 servings

- **Nonstick cooking spray, *Pam*®**
- **1 tablespoon extra virgin olive oil**
- **2 cups chopped yellow onions**
- **2 packages (6 ounces each) refrigerated oven-roasted diced chicken, *Tyson*®**
- **1 can (4-ounce) diced green chiles, *Ortega*®**
- **2 jars (16 ounces each) medium-hot green salsa, *Mrs. Renfro's*®**
- **4 cups tortilla chips, crumbled, *Tostitos*®**
- **2 cups grated 4-cheese Mexican cheese blend, *Sargento*®**
- **4 to 6 eggs**
- **2 tablespoons butter, cut into 4 to 6 pieces**
- **¼ cup chopped fresh cilantro**
- **1 container (8-ounce) sour cream**
- **2 teaspoons lime juice, *ReaLime*®**

1. Preheat oven to 450°F. Lightly spray a 9×13-inch baking dish with cooking spray; set aside.

2. In a large heavy ovenproof skillet, heat oil over high heat. Add 1½ cups of the onions; cook and stir about 5 minutes or until onions begin to soften. Add chicken and chiles; cook and stir 3 minutes. Stir in salsa. Simmer 3 minutes or just until heated through. Stir in chips. Transfer chicken mixture to prepared baking dish. Sprinkle with cheese and make shallow indentations for the eggs. Crack an egg into each indentation and place a piece of butter on each egg.

3. Bake about 10 minutes or just until cheese is melted and eggs are set. Sprinkle with remaining ½ cup onions and cilantro. Stir together sour cream and lime juice and serve on the side.

King Ranch Casserole

Prep 15 minutes **Bake** 50 minutes **Makes** 6 servings

- 3 **tablespoons butter**
- 1 **cup frozen chopped onions, *Ore-Ida*®**
- 3 **celery sticks, finely chopped, *Ready Pac*®**
- 1 **cup frozen chopped green bell peppers, *Pictsweet*®**
- 2 **packages (6 ounces each) frozen grilled chicken breast strips, chopped, *Foster Farms*®**
- 1 **can (10-ounce) diced tomatoes and green chiles, drained, *Ro-Tel*®**
- 1 **jar (2-ounce) chopped pimientos, *Dromedary*®**
- 1 **can (10.75-ounce) condensed cream of chicken soup, *Campbell's*®**
- 1 **can (10.75-ounce) condensed cream of mushroom soup, *Campbell's*®**
- 1 **can (10.75-ounce) condensed cheddar cheese soup, *Campbell's*®**
- 1 **bag (17.5-ounce) soft taco-size tortillas, cut in half then cut into strips, *Mission*®**
- 1 **cup shredded Monterey Jack cheese, *Kraft*®**
- **Hot pepper sauce, *Tabasco*® (optional)**

1. Preheat oven to 350°F. Grease the bottom of a 9×13-inch baking dish with 1 tablespoon of the butter and set aside.

2. In a large skillet, heat remaining 2 tablespoons of butter over medium heat. Add onions, celery, and green peppers; cook and stir until tender. Remove from heat and stir in the chopped chicken, diced tomatoes, and pimientos; set aside.

3. In a medium bowl, stir together soups until smooth. Pour one-third of the soup mixture into prepared baking dish. Place one-third of tortilla strips on soup. Top with half the chicken and vegetable mixture. Repeat layers, ending with chicken and vegetable mixture. Top with remaining third of tortilla strips and remaining third of sauce. Sprinkle cheese over top. Cover tightly with foil.

4. Bake for 35 minutes. Remove foil and bake for about 15 minutes more or until bubbling. Serve with hot pepper sauce (optional).

Turkey Tetrazzini Bake

Prep 20 minutes **Bake** 30 minutes **Makes** 4 servings

- ½ **pound spaghetti, broken in half**
- 2 **tablespoons butter**
- 1 **package (8-ounce) sliced mushrooms**
- 2 **teaspoons bottled garlic blend, *Gourmet Garden*®**
- 1 **can (10.5-ounce) white sauce**
- ¼ **cup half-and-half**
- 2 **tablespoons sherry**
- 1 **cup shredded Swiss cheese, *Sargento*®**
- 2 **cups cubed cooked turkey**
- ½ **cup shaved Parmesan cheese**
- ¼ **cup crumbled cooked bacon**

1. Preheat oven to 325°F. Spray a 2-quart casserole dish with cooking spray and set aside.

2. In a large pot of boiling salted water, cook spaghetti about 10 minutes or until tender but not al dente. Drain pasta and reserve ¼ cup pasta water.

3. In a large saucepan, melt butter over medium-high heat. Add mushrooms and garlic; cook and stir 6 minutes or until soft. Stir in white sauce, half-and-half, and sherry; heat through. Stir in Swiss cheese until melted. Remove from heat. Stir in cooked pasta, turkey, and ¼ cup of the reserved pasta water until well mixed. Transfer to prepared casserole dish. Sprinkle Parmesan cheese and bacon over top.

4. Bake for 30 to 35 minutes or until bubbling. Serve hot.

Crunchy Tuna Bake

Prep 25 minutes **Bake** 30 minutes **Makes** 6 servings

- 1 **package (12-ounce) medium egg noodles, *Manischewitz*®**
- 1 **cup frozen onions, celery, bell peppers, and parsley blend**
- 2 **tablespoons butter**
- 1 **package (8-ounce) sliced mushrooms**
- 1 **box (10-ounce) frozen chopped broccoli, thawed and drained**
- 1 **can (10.75-ounce) condensed cream of mushroom soup, *Campbell's*®**
- 1 **can (10.75-ounce) condensed golden mushroom soup, *Campbell's*®**
- ⅓ **cup half-and-half**
- 2 **cans (6 ounces each) chunk tuna in water, drained, *Bumble Bee*®**
- 2½ **cups shredded sharp cheddar cheese, *Kraft*®**
- **Salt and ground black pepper**
- 1½ **cups french-fried onions, *French's*®**

1. Preheat oven to 375°F. Spray a 9×13-inch baking dish with cooking spray.

2. In a large pot of boiling water, cook egg noodles about 8 minutes or until tender but not quite al dente. Drain and return to pot; set aside.

3. In a saucepan, cook vegetable blend in butter over medium-high heat until tender. Add mushrooms; cook for 8 minutes. Stir in broccoli. Transfer to pot.

4. Combine soups and half-and-half. Stir into pot. Stir in tuna and 2 cups cheese; season. Transfer to baking dish. Sprinkle with remaining cheese and onions.

5. Bake for 30 to 40 minutes or until heated through and browned.

One-Dish Dinners

The one-dish dinner is a busy cook's best friend. It simplifies cooking—and cleanup. When there's only one pot to wash, you're out of the kitchen fast to spend the evening doing something you love—taking a walk, reading, or watching a soccer game.

Barbecued Brisket
with Corn on the Cob and Potatoes

Prep 15 minutes **Bake** 3 hours + 45 minutes **Makes** 8 servings

- 2 **teaspoons ground black pepper**
- 1 **teaspoon kosher salt**
- 1 **4-pound beef brisket, trimmed of fat**
- 2 **tablespoons vegetable oil**
- 1½ **cups barbecue sauce, *Bulls-Eye®***
- 1½ **cups light beer, water, or beef broth**
- 1 **tablespoon bottled minced garlic, *Gourmet Garden®***
- 1 **tablespoon coarse-ground mustard, *Inglehoffer®***
- 1 **tablespoon cider vinegar**
- 1 **envelope onion soup mix, *Lipton®***
- 8 **frozen mini corn on the cob, thawed, *Green Giant® Nibblers®***
- 1 **bag (20-ounce) frozen roasted potatoes, thawed, *Ore-Ida®***

1. Preheat oven to 325°F. Rub the pepper and salt into the brisket.

2. In a Dutch oven or large pot, heat oil over medium-high heat. Cut brisket to fit Dutch oven, if necessary. Brown the brisket on all sides, in batches if more than one piece.

3. In a medium bowl, combine the barbecue sauce, beer, garlic, mustard, vinegar, and soup mix. Pour over the brisket, making sure to cover completely. Cover Dutch oven and place in oven. Bake for 3 hours.

4. Increase oven temperature to 400°F. Add the corn and potatoes to the Dutch oven. Bake, uncovered, for 45 minutes more. Remove meat and vegetables to platter; cover to keep warm. Strain sauce into a medium saucepan. Bring sauce to a boil; simmer sauce until thickened.

5. Slice brisket across the grain into thin strips; serve with corn, potatoes, and sauce.

Fricassee of Beef

Prep 15 minutes **Cook** 65 minutes **Makes** 4 servings

- 1 **pound beef stew meat**
- **Salt and ground black pepper**
- ¼ **cup all-purpose flour**
- 2 **tablespoons butter**
- 1 **package (14-ounce) frozen pearl onions,** ***C & W®***
- 1 **package (8-ounce) baby carrots**
- 1½ **cups reduced-sodium beef broth,** ***Swanson®***
- 1 **box (10-ounce) frozen Brussels sprouts, thawed and halved,** ***Bird's Eye®***
- 1 **packet (1.6-ounce) garlic and herb sauce mix,** ***Knorr®***
- 1 **container (21-ounce) refrigerated garlic mashed potatoes,** ***Country Crock®***

1. Season meat well with salt and pepper. Dredge in flour and shake off excess.

2. In a large skillet with a tight-fitting lid, melt butter. Add beef and brown on all sides. Add onions, carrots, and beef broth; bring to a boil. Cover and reduce heat to low. Simmer for 1 hour.

3. Remove lid and add halved Brussels sprouts. Increase heat to medium-high and bring to a boil. Stir in sauce mix. Simmer for 3 minutes or until sauce thickens. If sauce becomes too thick, thin with a little water. Meanwhile, microwave potatoes according to package directions.

4. Serve hot beef and vegetables over heated mashed potatoes.

Gravied Beef with Onions and Purple Potatoes

Prep 35 minutes **Cook** 1 hour **Makes** 4 servings

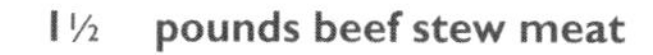

- 1½ **pounds beef stew meat**
- 2 **tablespoons steak rub,** ***McCormick® Grill Mates®***
- 3 **tablespoons extra virgin olive oil**
- 2 **cups frozen chopped onions,** ***Ore-Ida®***
- 2 **tablespoons bottled minced garlic,** ***Gourmet Garden®***
- 1 **jar (18-ounce) beef gravy,** ***Hunt's®***
- 1 **cup beef broth,** ***Swanson®***
- 2 **tablespoons tomato paste,** ***Hunt's®***
- 1½ **pounds purple potatoes, scrubbed and quartered**
- **Snipped fresh parsley**

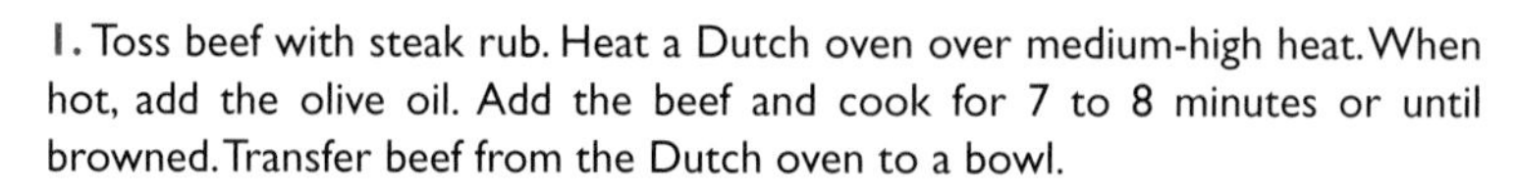

1. Toss beef with steak rub. Heat a Dutch oven over medium-high heat. When hot, add the olive oil. Add the beef and cook for 7 to 8 minutes or until browned. Transfer beef from the Dutch oven to a bowl.

2. Add the onions and garlic to the Dutch oven. Cook for 3 minutes, stirring frequently. Stir in the gravy, broth, and tomato paste. Add potatoes and beef, along with any juices in bowl. Bring to a boil, stirring frequently.

3. Reduce the heat to low. Cover the Dutch oven and simmer about 1 hour or until the meat is tender, stirring occasionally. Sprinkle with parsley and serve.

Mongolian Barbeque Stir-Fry

Start to Finish 25 minutes **Makes** 4 servings

SAUCE

- 3 **tablespoons teriyaki sauce,** ***Kikkoman®***
- 3 **tablespoons dry sherry**
- 2 **tablespoons light soy sauce,** ***Kikkoman®***
- 2 **tablespoons toasted sesame oil**
- 1 **tablespoon Asian chili sauce**
- 1 **tablespoon sugar**
- 1 **tablespoon bottled ginger puree,** ***Gourmet Garden®***
- 1 **tablespoon cornstarch**

STIR-FRY

- 1½ **pounds boneless beef top sirloin or tenderloin, thinly sliced across the grain**
- 2 **teaspoons kosher salt**
- 3 **tablespoons peanut oil or vegetable oil**
- 1 **package (14-ounce) frozen vegetable Japanese stir-fry blend,** ***Pictsweet®***
- **Cooked angel hair pasta or cooked jasmine rice**
- **Sesame oil**

1. For the sauce, in a small bowl, stir together all ingredients; set aside.

2. For the stir-fry, toss sliced steak with salt and set aside. Heat a wok over high heat about 1 minute or until hot. Heat 2 tablespoons of the peanut oil in wok. Add half the beef and stir-fry for 2 minutes or just until beef is cooked. Do not overcook. Remove beef to large bowl. Repeat with remaining beef and remove to bowl.

3. Reduce heat to medium-high. Heat remaining 1 tablespoon peanut oil in wok. Add mixed vegetables and stir-fry for 5 to 7 minutes or until vegetables are tender. Add the cooked beef and sauce to the wok. Cook and stir until sauce thickens and the beef is heated through.

4. Serve over angel hair pasta or rice drizzled with a little sesame oil.

Sweet-and-Sour Pork

Start to Finish 30 minutes **Makes** 4 servings

- 1 **pound pork tenderloin**
- 1 **box (8-ounce) tempura seafood batter mix, *McCormick*®**
- ¼ **cup vegetable oil**
- 1 **tablespoon bottled minced garlic, *Gourmet Garden*®**
- 1 **bag (16-ounce) Asian stir-fry vegetables, thawed, *C & W*®**
- 2 **tablespoons frozen orange juice concentrate, thawed, *Minute Maid*®**
- 1 **cup sweet-and-sour sauce, *Kikkoman*®**
- 1 **can (8-ounce) pineapple chunks in juice, *Dole*®**
- 1 **can (5-ounce) chow mein noodles, *La Choy*®**
- 1 **tablespoon sesame seeds (optional), *McCormick*®**
- **Light soy sauce, *Kikkoman*® (optional)**
- **Sweet hot mustard, *Inglehoffer*®**

1. Cut pork into 1-inch cubes. Toss with tempura mix, shaking off excess.

2. In a large skillet or wok, heat oil over high heat. When oil begins to shimmer, add pork and stir-fry until golden brown and cooked through. Remove with a slotted spoon to a plate lined with paper towels.

3. Add garlic to skillet and stir-fry about 30 seconds or until fragrant, stirring constantly. Add the vegetables and stir-fry about 4 minutes or until tender. Stir in the orange juice concentrate and sweet-and-sour sauce. Bring to a boil. Add the pork and the pineapple chunks with juice. Return to a boil, stirring constantly until thickened.

4. Arrange chow mein noodles on individual serving plates and spoon pork over noodles. Sprinkle sesame seeds (optional) over each serving; serve with soy sauce (optional) and sweet hot mustard.

Pork Chops with Apples and Winter Squash

Start to Finish 30 minutes **Makes** 4 servings

- 4 **boneless pork chops, cut about ¾ inch thick, trimmed**
- 1 **tablespoon Montreal chicken seasoning, *McCormick® Grill Mates®***
- 1 **tablespoon extra virgin olive oil**
- 1 **medium yellow onion, thinly sliced**
- 1 **box (12-ounce) frozen winter squash, thawed, *Birds Eye®***
- 1 **can (10.75-ounce) condensed cream of celery soup, *Campbell's®***
- 1 **cup reduced-sodium chicken broth**
- ¾ **cup apple cider, *Tree Top®***
- 1 **teaspoon Dijon mustard**
- 1 **teaspoon dried thyme, *McCormick®***
- 2 **packages (2.4 ounces each) tart apples, *Chiquita®***

1. Season chops with chicken seasoning.

2. Heat a large ovenproof skillet over medium-high heat; when hot, add the oil. Add chops and brown about 4 minutes per side. Transfer chops to a plate.

3. Add onion to the skillet. Cook for 2 to 3 minutes or until slices begin to soften, stirring often. Add the squash. Cover and cook for 3 to 5 minutes or until barely heated through, stirring occasionally. Stir in the condensed soup, broth, cider, and mustard. Add the thyme, rubbing it between your fingers as you add it to the pan. Return pork chops to pan and top with the apples. Bring to a boil; reduce heat to low. Cover and cook for 10 minutes.

Spicy Italian Sausage Bake

Prep 15 minutes **Bake** 35 minutes **Makes** 4 servings

- 4 **spicy Italian sausages, casings removed, *Papa Cantella's®***
- 2 **boxes (10 ounces each) frozen leaf spinach, *C&sW®***
- 1 **cup ricotta cheese, *Precious®***
- ½ **cup condensed cream of mushroom soup, *Campbell's®***
- 1½ **teaspoons bottled chopped garlic, *Gourmet Garden®***
- ½ **teaspoon all-purpose seasoning, *McCormick***
- ¼ **teaspoon red pepper flakes, *McCormick®***
- 1 **jar (2-ounce) sliced pimientos, drained, *Dromedary®***
- ¾ **cup french-fried onions, *French's®***

1. Preheat oven to 350°F. Spray a 2-quart casserole with cooking spray.

2. In a large skillet, brown sausage over medium heat, breaking up pieces as it cooks. Drain and set aside.

3. Heat spinach in a microwave-safe bowl for 3 minutes. Squeeze out excess water. Wipe bowl dry. Stir together ricotta cheese, soup, garlic, seasoning, and pepper flakes. Stir in sausage, spinach, and pimientos. Transfer to dish. Bake for 30 minutes. Sprinkle onions over the top; bake 5 minutes more.

Chicken Pesto Pot Pie

Prep 15 minutes **Bake** 15 minutes **Stand** 10 minutes **Makes** 6 servings

- **Nonstick cooking spray, *Pam*®**
- 2 **tablespoons butter**
- ¼ **cup roasted red bell pepper, drained and chopped, *Marzetti*®**
- 1 **tablespoon gravy flour, *Wondra*®**
- 1 **teaspoon Montreal chicken seasoning, *McCormick*® *Grill Mates*®**
- 1 **bag (16-ounce) frozen mixed vegetables, thawed, *Birds Eye*®**
- 1 **can (10.75-ounce) condensed cream of celery soup, *Campbell's*®**
- 2 **cups chopped deli rotisserie chicken**
- 1 **cup half-and-half or light cream**
- ½ **cup grated Parmesan cheese, *DiGiorno*®**
- 1 **packet (0.5-ounce) pesto sauce mix, *Knorr*®**
- 1 **tube (11-ounce) refrigerated garlic breadstick dough, *Pillsbury*®**

1. Preheat oven to 425°F. Spray a 9-inch deep-dish pie plate with cooking spray; set side.

2. In a large saucepan, melt butter over medium heat. Add the chopped pepper, flour, and chicken seasoning. Cook for 30 seconds, stirring constantly. Add vegetables and cream of celery soup. Bring to a boil; reduce heat. Cook and stir about 5 minutes or until thickened. Remove from heat. Stir in chicken, half-and-half, Parmesan cheese, and pesto mix. Pour the mixture into the pie plate and spread evenly.

3. Unroll and separate the breadstick dough, leaving the short ends connected. Starting at the edge of the dish, wind strips in concentric circles over chicken mixture.

4. Bake for 15 minutes or until the bread is golden and the sauce is bubbling. Remove from oven and let stand for 10 minutes before serving.

Note: If you have any leftover breadstick dough, tie the extra pieces in knots, bake, and serve with the pot pie.

Thai Green Curry Chicken with Baby Corn

Start to Finish 30 minutes **Makes** 6 servings

- 3 **tablespoons vegetable oil**
- 2 **tablespoons + 2 teaspoons bottled minced ginger blend, *Gourmet Garden®***
- 1 **tablespoon bottled crushed garlic blend, *Gourmet Garden®***
- 1 **package (8-ounce) sliced mushrooms**
- ½ **cup sliced scallions (green onions)**
- 1¼ **pounds boneless, skinless chicken breasts, cut into 1-inch pieces**
- 1 **cup + 2 tablespoons light coconut milk, *Thai Kitchen®***
- 1 **cup reduced-sodium chicken broth, *Swanson®***
- 2 **to 3 tablespoons green curry paste, *Thai Kitchen®***
- 1 **pound fresh snow peas, rinsed, stems removed**
- 1 **can (15-ounce) baby corn, each ear cut diagonally into thirds**
- 2 **packages (8.8 ounces each) precooked roasted chicken rice, *Uncle Ben's® Ready Rice***
- **Fresh cilantro sprigs (optional)**

1. Preheat oven to 170°F.

2. In a large skillet or wok, heat oil over high heat. When the oil starts to shimmer, add 2 tablespoons ginger and the garlic, stirring until fragrant, about 30 seconds. Add the mushrooms and scallions; cook for 3 minutes, stirring constantly. Add the chicken; cook about 5 minutes or until the chicken is no longer pink, stirring occasionally.

3. Add 1 cup of the coconut milk, chicken broth, and curry paste. Bring to a boil and add the snow peas and baby corn. Reduce heat to medium and simmer for 10 minutes.

4. Heat rice in microwave according to package directions. Carefully empty rice into a bowl and stir in remaining 2 tablespoons coconut milk and remaining 2 teaspoons ginger.

5. Serve chicken hot over rice with cilantro (optional).

Tip: Have all your ingredients prepped and ready to go. The cooking in this dish happens very fast.

Slow-Cooked Greek Chicken

4-quart slow cooker **Prep** 5 minutes **Cook** 6 to 8 hours (low) **Makes** 4 servings

- **8 boneless, skinless chicken thighs**
- **1 teaspoon salt**
- **2 teaspoons Greek seasoning, *McCormick*®**
- **1½ cups frozen chopped onions, *Ore-Ida*®**
- **1 can (10.75-ounce) condensed cream of chicken soup, *Campbell's*®**
- **1 can (14.5-ounce) diced tomatoes with basil, garlic, and oregano, drained, *Del Monte*®**
- **1 can (3.8-ounce) sliced black olives, *Early California*®**
- **2 tablespoons frozen lemon juice, thawed, *Minute Maid*®**
- **Hot cooked rice**

1. Season chicken with salt and Greek seasoning. In the slow cooker, place onions, then top with chicken. In a bowl, stir together soup, tomatoes, and olives; pour over chicken.

2. Cover and cook on low for 6 to 8 hours. Stir in lemon juice. Serve hot over hot cooked rice.

Smothered Chicken

Prep 20 minutes **Roast** 45 minutes **Makes** 6 servings

- ½ **cup mayonnaise, *Best Foods®/ Hellmann's®***
- 1 **tablespoon French herb roasting rub, *McCormick®***
- ½ **teaspoon garlic salt, *McCormick®***
- 3 **pounds meaty chicken pieces (breast halves, thighs, and drumsticks)**
- 4 **large shallots, peeled and sliced**
- 1 **tablespoon extra virgin olive oil**
- 2 **cups dry white wine**
- ½ **cup heavy cream**
- 1 **package (1.6-ounce) garlic and herb sauce mix, *Knorr®***
- **Salt and ground black pepper**

1. Preheat oven to 375°F.

2. In a bowl, stir together mayonnaise, herb rub, and garlic salt; liberally brush on chicken pieces. Place chicken in a shallow roasting pan. Toss sliced shallots with olive oil and scatter around chicken.

3. Roast for 45 to 55 minutes or until chicken is no longer pink at the bone and juices run clear (170°F for breasts; 180°F for thighs and drumsticks). Transfer chicken to a serving platter; loosely tent with foil to keep warm. Leave shallots in roasting pan.

4. Place roasting pan on range top over medium-high heat. Deglaze pan with wine and reduce by half. Stir in cream and sauce mix. Bring to a boil; reduce heat. Simmer about 3 minutes or until thickened, stirring occasionally. Season to taste with salt and pepper. Spoon hot sauce over chicken.

Orzo Turkey à la Piccata

Start to Finish 25 minutes **Makes** 4 servings

- 1 cup orzo pasta, *Barilla*®
- 1½ cups diced leftover cooked vegetables
- ½ cup white wine
- 6 tablespoons butter
- ¾ cup reduced-sodium chicken broth, *Swanson*®
- 3 tablespoons frozen lemon juice, thawed, *Minute Maid*®
- 1 teaspoon bottled garlic puree, *Gourmet Garden*®
- 2 cups cooked turkey strips
- 2 tablespoons capers, drained
- 2 tablespoons finely chopped parsley

1. In a pot of boiling salted water, cook orzo according to package directions. Drain and return orzo to pot. Cover to keep warm.

2. Place vegetables in a small microwave-safe bowl. Microwave, covered, on high for 1 to 2 minutes. Add vegetables to orzo in pot.

3. While pasta cooks, in a large skillet, reduce wine to 2 tablespoons over medium-high heat. Reduce heat to medium and add butter. Once butter melts, stir in broth, lemon juice, and garlic. Add turkey and heat for 3 to 4 minutes or until heated through. Stir in capers and parsley. Remove from heat.

4. Serve turkey over hot vegetable orzo.

Chicken Fried Steak with Southern Gravy

Prep 35 minutes **Cook** 1 hour **Makes** 4 servings

- 1 cup all-purpose flour
- 2 packets (1 ounce each) dry ranch dressing mix, *Hidden Valley*®
- Salt and pepper
- 3 cups buttermilk
- 1 egg, lightly beaten
- 1 pound cubed steak, cut into 4 pieces
- Oil, for frying
- 1 cup chicken broth, *Swanson*®
- 1 packet (2.64-ounce) country gravy mix, *McCormick*®
- Mashed potatoes

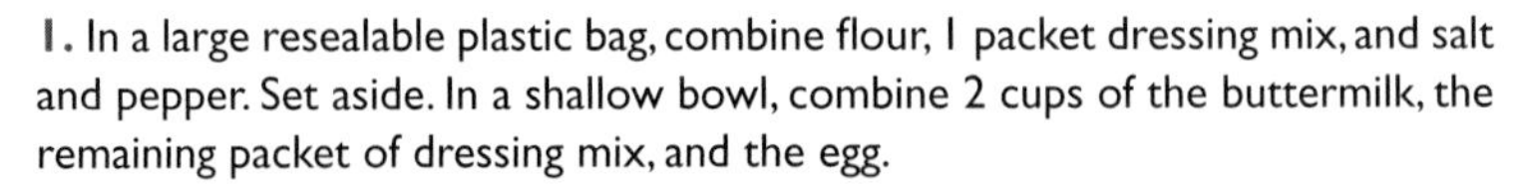

1. In a large resealable plastic bag, combine flour, 1 packet dressing mix, and salt and pepper. Set aside. In a shallow bowl, combine 2 cups of the buttermilk, the remaining packet of dressing mix, and the egg.

2. Soak steaks in buttermilk mixture. Remove 1 steak, letting excess buttermilk mixture drip off. Add to flour mixture, seal bag, and toss to coat. Shake off any excess flour and dip again in the buttermilk mixture. Return to flour mixture, seal bag, and toss; set aside. Repeat process for remaining steaks.

3. In a large cast-iron skillet, heat ½ inch oil to 350°F. Fry 2 steaks in the pan at a time for 4 minutes per side or until golden brown. Drain on paper towels.

4. For gravy, in a small saucepan, combine remaining 1 cup buttermilk, broth, and gravy mix. Bring to a simmer and stir well. Spoon over steaks and potatoes.

From the Oven

"Nothing says loving like something from the oven" may really refer to baked goods, but in my book, it also refers to roasted dinners that fill the house with delicious smells as they cook. One of the most beautiful things about oven dinners is that—unlike dishes you cook on the stovetop—you can walk away for a while and come back to food that's ready to put on the table.

Salt Free

Beefy Pot Roast
with Yorkshire Pudding

Prep 15 minutes **Chill** 1 hour **Roast** 4¼ hours **Bake** 20 minutes **Makes** 6 servings

YORKSHIRE PUDDING

- 1 cup baking mix, *Pioneer*®
- 3 eggs
- 1 cup whole milk

ROAST

- 2 pounds beef top sirloin roast
- ¼ cup all-purpose flour
- 1 package (0.75-ounce) mushroom gravy mix, *McCormick*®
- 1 teaspoon ground black pepper
- 4 tablespoons extra virgin olive oil
- ½ cup frozen chopped onions, thawed, *Ore-Ida*®
- 1 tablespoon bottled garlic blend, *Gourmet Garden*®
- 2 large carrots, chopped
- 2 stalks celery, with tops, chopped
- 1 bay leaf, *McCormick*®
- ½ teaspoon dried thyme, *McCormick*®
- 2 cans (10.5 ounces each) beef consommé, *Campbell's*®
- ½ cup red wine
- 2 tablespoons low-sodium soy sauce, *Kikkoman*®
- 1 package (8-ounce) small button mushrooms, brushed clean

1. For the Yorkshire pudding, in a small bowl, stir together the baking mix, eggs, and milk until smooth. Cover and refrigerate for at least 1 hour.

2. For the roast, preheat the oven to 450°F. In a shallow dish, combine the flour, 1½ tablespoons of the mushroom gravy mix, and the pepper; press seasonings into the meat, shaking off any excess. Discard remaining flour mixture.

3. In a heavy skillet, heat 2 tablespoons of the olive oil over medium-high heat. Brown the roast on both sides, about 5 to 6 minutes.

4. In a 6-quart Dutch oven, heat the remaining 2 tablespoons olive oil over medium-high heat. Add the onions and garlic; cook about 5 minutes, stirring often. Add the carrots, celery, bay leaf, and thyme; cook and stir for 5 minutes more. Add the consommé, red wine, soy sauce, and the remaining gravy mix. Add the meat and sprinkle the mushrooms over all. Put the lid on Dutch oven.

5. Roast for 15 minutes. Reduce oven temperature to 225°F. Roast for 4 hours. Remove from oven.

6. Turn the oven temperature up to 450°F. Remove roast from the Dutch oven and slice. Remove gravy, leaving 1 cup in the Dutch oven. Return sliced beef to the Dutch oven; pour remaining gravy over beef.

7. When the oven reaches 450°F, remove the batter from the refrigerator and pour over the surface of the roast. Bake, uncovered, for 20 to 25 minutes or until the pudding is puffed and golden. Serve at once.

Bam Bam Beef Ribs

Prep 15 minutes **Marinate** 15 minutes **Roast** 1½ hours **Stand** 10 minutes **Makes** 4 servings

- 4 pounds meaty beef back ribs
- ¼ cup + 2 teaspoons steak rub, *McCormick® Grill Mates®*
- 1 cup ketchup, *Heinz®*
- ¼ cup apricot preserves, *Knott's®*
- ¼ cup packed brown sugar, *C&H®*
- 2 tablespoons chili-garlic sauce, *Lee Kum Kee®*
- 1 habañero chile, seeded and minced
- 2 tablespoons red wine vinegar, *Pompeian®*

1. Preheat oven to 450°F. Line a rimmed baking sheet with aluminum foil; set aside. Cut ribs into individual portions. Place on baking sheet and coat ribs with the ¼ cup steak rub. Let stand for 15 minutes.

2. Roast ribs for 30 minutes.

3. Meanwhile, in a small saucepan, combine remaining 2 teaspoons steak rub, ketchup, apricot preserves, brown sugar, chili-garlic sauce, habañero chile, and vinegar. Bring to a boil. Reduce heat and simmer for 5 minutes. Keep warm.

4. Remove ribs from oven and reduce oven temperature to 325°F. Allow enough time for oven to cool to temperature.

5. Liberally brush ribs with sauce and return to oven. Continue roasting for 1 hour, basting with sauce after 30 minutes. Remove from oven and brush on remaining sauce. Let stand for 10 minutes before serving.

BBQ Tri-Tip Roast

Prep 15 minutes **Marinate** 12 to 18 hours **Stand** 30 minutes + 15 minutes **Bake** 30 minutes **Makes** 4 servings

- 1 2-pound beef tri-tip roast, trimmed
- 1 tablespoon Montreal steak seasoning, *McCormick® Grill Mates®*
- 1 cup bourbon, *Jim Beam®*
- ¼ cup cracked peppercorn herb roasting rub, *McCormick®*
- 1 teaspoon ground chipotle chile pepper, *McCormick®*
- 1 teaspoon hickory-flavored liquid smoke, *Wright's®*
- 2 medium yellow onions, thinly sliced
- 1 bottle (18-ounce) hickory barbecue sauce, heated, *Bulls-Eye®*

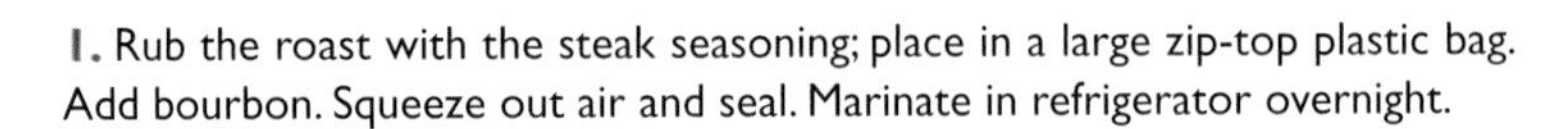

1. Rub the roast with the steak seasoning; place in a large zip-top plastic bag. Add bourbon. Squeeze out air and seal. Marinate in refrigerator overnight.

2. Preheat oven to 375°F. Remove the meat from the marinade and pat the meat dry. In a small bowl, stir together the herb roasting rub and chile pepper. Rub roast with liquid smoke and pat spice mixture into the meat. Let roast stand at room temperature for 30 minutes.

3. Place the meat and onions in a 9×13-inch baking dish. Cover with foil and bake for 20 to 25 minutes or until an instant-read thermometer inserted in thickest part of roast registers 125°F.

4. Remove foil and bake for 10 to 15 minutes more or until browned and an instant-read thermometer inserted in thickest part of roast registers 135°F for medium rare. Remove from oven and cover with foil; let stand for 15 minutes before slicing. Slice roast across the grain. Arrange meat slices on a platter with roasted onions from pan. Serve with heated barbecue sauce.

Herbed Pork Roast with Garlicky Buttermilk Mashed Potatoes

Prep 5 minutes **Roast** 1¼ hours **Stand** 10 minutes **Makes** 4 servings

- 1 **tablespoon garlic herb seasoning blend, *McCormick®***
- 1 **tablespoon fines herbes, *McCormick®***
- 1 **tablespoon bottled garlic blend, *Gourmet Garden®***
- 1 **tablespoon frozen lemon juice, thawed, *Minute Maid®***
- 1 **2½-pound boneless pork top loin roast**

1. Preheat oven to 450°F.

2. For the pork roast, in a small bowl, stir together garlic herb seasoning, fines herbs, garlic, and lemon juice until well combined. Rub over pork roast and place roast in a shallow roasting pan.

3. Place roast in oven and reduce oven temperature to 325°F. Roast about 1¼ hours or until an instant-read thermometer inserted in roast registers 150°F. Remove from oven; let stand for 10 minutes before slicing. Serve with mashed potatoes.

Garlicky Buttermilk Mashed Potatoes: Cook 1 (24-ounce) bag *Ore-Ida® Steam n' Mash®* frozen cut russet potatoes in microwave according to package directions. Mash with ⅔ cup buttermilk, 2 tablespoons butter, 2 teaspoons bottled garlic blend, and salt and pepper to taste.

Braised Baby Back Ribs

Prep 5 minutes **Marinate** 30 minutes **Bake** 3 hours + 15 minutes **Makes** 4 servings

- 2 **slabs pork baby back ribs, cut into individual portions**
- ¼ **cup pork rub, *McCormick® Grill Mates®***
- 2 **tablespoons vegetable oil**
- 2 **envelopes dry onion soup mix, *Lipton®***
- 5 **cans (12 ounces each) soda, *Dr Pepper®***
- 1 **bottle (18-ounce) barbecue sauce, *Bulls-Eye®***

1. Preheat oven to 300°F. Coat ribs with pork rub; let stand at room temperature for 30 minutes. In a large skillet, heat oil over medium-high heat. Working in batches, brown meaty sides of ribs in hot oil. Arrange ribs in two 9×13-inch pans, meaty sides down. Sprinkle 1 envelope of onion soup mix over each pan of ribs. Pour 2½ cans of soda into each pan. Cover pans with foil.

2. Bake for 3 hours, checking occasionally to be sure liquid doesn't completely evaporate. Transfer ribs to a rimmed baking sheet, meaty sides up. Set aside. Reserve braising liquid; skim off fat. Increase oven temperature to 375°F.

3. In a medium saucepan, bring barbecue sauce and 1 cup of the reserved braising liquid to a boil. Reduce heat; simmer about 15 minutes or until thickened. Brush ribs with some of the barbecue sauce and bake in oven for 15 minutes. Cut into serving-size portions. Serve ribs hot with extra sauce.

Stuffed Pork Tenderloin with Red Wine Sauce

Prep 30 minutes **Roast** 20 minutes **Stand** 10 minutes **Makes** 4 servings

PORK

- 1 1½-pound pork tenderloin
- 2 tablespoons French herb roasting rub, *McCormick*®
- 1 package (3-ounce) prosciutto
- 4 to 6 sticks string cheese
- 2 tablespoons extra virgin olive oil

WINE SAUCE

- 1 cup dry red wine
- 2 tablespoons butter, cubed
- ¼ teaspoon white or cider vinegar

1. Preheat oven to 425°F. Spray a baking sheet with cooking spray; set aside.

2. Remove any silver skin from tenderloin. Make a lengthwise slit, being careful not to cut all the way through the meat. Spread open the meat and season both sides with rub. Wrap a prosciutto slice around each cheesestick. Lay wrapped cheese along center of tenderloin. Tie tenderloin closed at 1-inch intervals with 100%-cotton kitchen string; use toothpicks to close ends.

3. In a large skillet, heat oil over medium heat. Brown the tenderloin for 6 to 8 minutes, turning often. When lightly browned, transfer meat to baking sheet. Roast for 20 to 30 minutes or until an instant-read thermometer inserted into the thickest part of tenderloin (not the cheese) registers 155°F. Remove from oven and let stand 10 minutes. Slice meat; arrange on platter or plates.

4. Add wine to skillet. Bring to a boil. Cook until wine is reduced to ½ cup. Remove from heat; stir in butter. Add vinegar. Drizzle over and around sliced meat.

Pork Chops Stuffed with Spinach and Ricotta

Prep 30 minutes **Bake** 15 minutes **Makes** 4 servings

- 4 bone-in pork rib chops, cut 1½ inches thick
- Salt and ground black pepper
- 1¼ cups shredded 4-cheese blend, *Sargento*®
- ½ cup ricotta cheese
- 2 tablespoons grated Asiago cheese, *Sargento*®
- 1 package (10-ounce) frozen spinach, thawed and squeezed dry
- ¼ cup plain bread crumbs
- 2 teaspoons Italian seasoning, *McCormick*®
- 2 teaspoons bottled crushed garlic, *Gourmet Garden*®
- 2 tablespoons vegetable oil

1. Preheat oven to 450°F. Cut a slit in each pork chop along the fatty long side of the chop, leaving three sides intact. Season with salt and pepper.

2. For stuffing, in a medium bowl, mix together the cheeses. Add spinach, bread crumbs, Italian seasoning, and garlic, mixing well. Season to taste with salt and pepper. Stuff each chop with stuffing. Close chop; secure with wooden picks if needed.

3. In a large ovenproof skillet, heat oil over medium-high heat. Cook chops, without moving, 3 minutes or until browned. Turn; cook 3 minutes more or until browned. Transfer skillet to oven; bake 15 to 20 minutes or until a thermometer inserted into center of stuffing registers 140°F, turning chops halfway through baking.

Roast Chicken
with Mushroom Glaze

Prep 10 minutes **Roast** 2 hours 5 minutes **Stand** 10 minutes **Makes** 6 servings

- **1** **3- to 4-pound roasting chicken**
- **1** **tablespoon kosher salt**
- **2** **teaspoons coarsely ground black pepper**
- **1** **package (8-ounce) whole button baby bella mushrooms**
- **3** **tablespoons bottled minced garlic, *Gourmet Garden*®**
- **1** **package (0.75-ounce) mushroom gravy mix, *McCormick*®**
- **¼** **cup honey**

1. Preheat oven to 450°F.

2. Rub chicken with the salt and pepper. Toss the mushrooms with 2 tablespoons of the garlic and stuff them into the bird. Tie legs together with 100%-cotton kitchen string. Place chicken on a wire rack in a large roasting pan. Roast chicken for 15 minutes. Reduce oven temperature to 325°F. Roast chicken for 20 minutes more.

3. For the glaze, while the chicken is roasting, in a small bowl, combine the gravy mix, honey, and the remaining garlic. Brush glaze over chicken. Roast for 1½ to 2 hours more or until an instant-read thermometer inserted in the meaty part of the thigh registers 180°F, brushing with glaze every 30 minutes.

4. Transfer chicken to a carving board and let stand for 10 minutes. Cut string from legs and spoon the mushrooms into a bowl. Carve the bird and serve.

Crispy Parmesan and Onion Crusted Chicken

Prep 15 minutes **Bake** 30 minutes **Makes** 4 servings

- **3** **cups french-fried onions, *French's*®**
- **½** **cup grated Parmesan cheese, *DiGiorno*®**
- **4** **tablespoons mayonnaise, *Best Foods*®/*Hellmann's*®**
- **1** **tablespoon Italian seasoning, *McCormick*®**
- **2** **tablespoon Dijon mustard, *Grey Poupon*®**
- **8** **boneless, skinless chicken thighs**

1. Preheat oven to 350°F. Lightly spray a baking sheet with nonstick cooking spray; set aside.

2. In a food processor, combine fried onions and Parmesan cheese. Pulse until finely ground. Transfer to a plate and set aside.

3. In a small bowl, stir together mayonnaise, Italian seasoning, and mustard. Coat chicken with mayonnaise mixture, then press chicken pieces into fried onions. Place on prepared baking sheet. Bake about 35 minutes or until an instant-read thermometer inserted into thigh registers 180°F. Serve hot.

Creamy Chicken Cobbler

Prep 10 minutes **Bake** 25 minutes **Makes** 4 servings

- **2** **tablespoons butter, melted**
- **1** **can (10.75-ounce) condensed cream of chicken soup, *Campbell's*®**
- **1** **jar (12-ounce) classic chicken gravy, *Heinz*®**
- **2** **cups chopped deli-cooked rotisserie chicken**
- **1** **bag (16-ounce) frozen mixed vegetables, thawed, *C&W*®**
- **3** **teaspoons Montreal chicken seasoning, *McCormick*® *Grill Mates*®**
- **1** **cup baking mix, *Bisquick*®**
- **1½** **cups milk**

1. Preheat oven to 400°F. Spread melted butter in the bottom of a 9×13-inch baking dish.

2. In a large saucepan, stir together soup, gravy, chicken, vegetables, and 2 teaspoons of the chicken seasoning. Heat through; remove from heat. Meanwhile, stir together baking mix, milk, and remaining 1 teaspoon chicken seasoning until smooth. Pour batter into prepared baking dish. Spoon chicken mixture over batter.

3. Bake for 25 to 30 minutes or until golden and bubbling. Serve hot.

Turkey Breast with Cinnamon Apples

Prep 20 minutes **Grill** 1¾ hours **Stand** 10 minutes **Makes** 12 servings

TURKEY

- ½ cup butter, softened
- 1 tablespoon Montreal chicken seasoning, *McCormick® Grill Mates®*
- 1 packet (0.74-ounce) spiced cider drink mix, *Alpine®*
- 2 teaspoons bottled crushed garlic, *Gourmet Garden®*
- 1 4- to 6-pound whole bone-in turkey breast
- Maple wood chips, soaked in water for at least 30 minutes

CINNAMON APPLES

- 6 Granny Smith apples, cored and quartered
- ⅓ cup packed brown sugar
- ⅓ cup chopped pecans
- ⅓ cup golden raisins
- 3 tablespoons butter
- 1 teaspoon ground cinnamon, *McCormick®*

1. Set up grill for indirect cooking over medium heat (no direct heat source under turkey). Oil grate when ready to cook.

2. In a small bowl, stir together butter, chicken seasoning, cider mix, and garlic with a fork. Loosen skin of turkey breast around the neck and work your hands under the skin, leaving the skin attached at the edges. Rub most of the butter under the skin and rub some over the skin as well.

3. For cinnamon apples, place quartered apples on a large piece of heavy-duty aluminum foil. In a small bowl, stir together brown sugar, pecans, raisins, butter, and cinnamon with a fork. Sprinkle over apples and wrap in foil. Crimp the edges of the packet so it won't leak.

4. Add soaked wood chips to smoke box if using a gas grill or place chips on hot coals if using charcoal. Place breast, skin side up, on hot oiled grill over a drip pan. Cover grill. Cook for 1¾ to 2¼ hours or until an instant-read thermometer inserted in thickest part of breast away from the bone registers 170°F.

5. During the last 30 minutes of cooking, add foil pouch of apples to grill. Turn pouch after 15 minutes. If using a charcoal grill, add 10 more briquettes and some soaked wood chips to each pile of coals after 1 hour.

6. Transfer turkey to a platter and let stand for 10 minutes. Slice and serve hot with cinnamon apples.

Indoor Method: Preheat oven to 325°F. Prepare turkey breast as directed. For a smoked flavor, add ¼ teaspoon liquid smoke to butter mixture. Place in roasting pan and roast for 1½ to 2¼ hours or until an instant-read thermometer inserted in thickest part of breast registers 170°F. Prepare apples as directed without foil pouch and add to roasting pan during the last 30 minutes of roasting.

Fennel Side of Salmon
with Veggie Mix

Prep 15 minutes **Bake** 25 minutes **Makes** 4 servings

- 1 **1½- to 2-pound salmon fillet**
- 1 **teaspoon kosher salt**
- 2 **teaspoons bottled minced garlic, *Gourmet Garden*®**
- 1 **whole fennel bulb, thinly sliced, green leafy tops reserved**
- 1 **package (19-ounce) frozen seasoned vegetable medley, *Green Giant*®**
- 4 **tablespoons unsalted butter, cut into 8 pieces**

1. Preheat oven to 375°F. Line a rimmed baking sheet with long sheets of foil, leaving enough extending beyond the sides to seal the salmon over the top.

2. Rinse the salmon and pat dry thoroughly with paper towels. Rub the salmon with the salt and place, skin side down, on the foil-lined baking sheet. Using the back of a spoon, spread garlic evenly on the fish. Top with the sliced fennel and frozen vegetables. Top the vegetables with the butter. Wrap the foil loosely around the salmon, sealing tightly so no steam will escape and leaving room for air to circulate inside.

3. Bake for 25 to 35 minutes or until salmon flakes easily when tested with a fork. Place the foil-wrapped salmon on a platter and unveil it tableside. Serve immediately.

Roasted Halibut
with Roasted Roots

Start to Finish 35 minutes **Makes** 4 servings

- **Nonstick olive oil cooking spray, *Pam*®**
- **4 medium red potatoes, peeled and cut into wedges**
- **2 medium rutabagas, peeled and cut into wedges**
- **2 small turnips, peeled and cut into wedges**
- **2 small yellow onions, peeled and cut into wedges**
- **3 cups frozen sliced carrots, thawed, *Birds Eye*®**
- **1 tablespoon bottled garlic blend, *Gourmet Garden*®**
- **1 teaspoon kosher salt**
- **¾ teaspoon ground black pepper**
- **1 package (1.6-ounce) garlic and herb sauce mix, *Knorr*®**
- **1 cup milk**
- **2 large lemons, thinly sliced**
- **4 6- to 8-ounce halibut fillets**
- **2 tablespoons extra virgin olive oil**

1. Preheat oven to 500°F. Spray two baking pans with cooking spray.

2. On one baking pan, combine potatoes, rutabagas, turnips, onions, carrots, and garlic. Spray with cooking spray and toss with half the salt and pepper. Reduce the oven temperature to 400°F. Roast for 15 minutes, stirring occasionally. Roast for 15 to 20 minutes more or until vegetables are tender.

3. While vegetables are roasting, in a medium saucepan, whisk the sauce mix into the milk. Bring to a boil over high heat. Reduce heat to low and simmer about 2 minutes or until thickened, stirring occasionally. Keep sauce warm.

4. Place lemon slices on the second baking pan. Arrange the fish on lemon slices; sprinkle fish with remaining salt and pepper. Drizzle olive oil over fish. Roast for 10 to 12 minutes or until fish flakes easily when tested with a fork.

5. Arrange the vegetables on serving plates and using a spatula, transfer the fish and lemon slices to the plates. Spoon warm sauce over fish. Serve immediately.

Desserts

Something sweet served with a glass of milk or a cup of coffee or tea is a sure way to bring smiles. Find a treat for every occasion in this collection of desserts, from a decadent four-layer cake suited to a special celebration to a warm and gooey cherry and chocolate crumble made for any mood, any day of the week.

Dad's Black and White Decadence

Prep 25 minutes **Bake** 29 minutes **Makes** 12 servings

- **Nonstick cooking spray for baking, *Pam®***
- 1 **box (18.25-ounce) chocolate cake mix, *Betty Crocker®***
- 3 **eggs**
- 1⅓ **cups low-fat chocolate milk, *Nestlé® Quik®***
- ½ **cup vegetable oil**
- 2 **teaspoons almond extract, *McCormick®***
- 1 **can (16-ounce) dark chocolate frosting, *Betty Crocker®***
- 1½ **cans (16 ounces each) butter cream frosting, *Betty Crocker®***
- 1 **cup semisweet or milk chocolate chips, *Nestlé®***
- 1 **cup white chocolate chips, *Nestlé®***

1. Preheat oven to 350°F. Lightly spray two 8-inch square cake pans with baking spray; set aside.

2. In a large mixing bowl, beat cake mix, eggs, chocolate milk, oil, and 1 teaspoon of the almond extract with an electric mixer on low for 30 seconds. Scrape down sides of bowl and beat on medium for 2 minutes. Spread batter in prepared pans.

3. Bake for 29 to 34 minutes or until a tester comes away clean and cakes start to pull away from the sides of the pans. Cool in pans for 5 minutes; remove cakes from pans and cool on wire racks.

4. Stir ½ teaspoon of the remaining almond extract into chocolate frosting. Stir remaining almond extract into the butter cream frosting. Level the cakes if they have crowned and split each layer horizontally with a serrated knife. Layer the cakes, spreading chocolate frosting between each. Frost the outside of the cake with the butter cream frosting. To finish the cake, alternately press the chocolate and white chocolate chips into the sides of the cake.

Peanut Butter and Pretzel Refrigerated Cake

Prep 15 minutes **Chill** 20 minutes + 4 hours **Makes** 8 servings

- **Nonstick cooking spray for baking, *Pam*®**
- 3 **cups mini pretzels, *Snyder's*® *of Hanover***
- 1 **tablespoon unsweetened cocoa powder, *Hershey's*®**
- ¼ **cup sugar**
- 1 **stick (½ cup) butter, melted**
- ¾ **cup chocolate topping, *Mrs. Richardson's*®**
- 1 **jar (7-ounce) marshmallow creme, *Kraft*®**
- ¾ **cup creamy peanut butter, *Skippy*® *Natural***
- 1 **container (8-ounce) whipped topping, thawed, *Cool Whip*®**
- **Mini pretzels, *Snyder's*® *of Hanover***
- **Crushed peanut brittle**

1. Spray an 8-inch springform pan with baking spray; set aside.

2. In a food processor, combine pretzels, cocoa powder, and sugar; pulse to fine crumbs. Add melted butter; pulse until mixture comes together. Press mixture into bottom of cake pan.

3. Place chocolate topping in a microwave-safe bowl. Microwave for 30 seconds or until warm. Pour over pretzel crust. Chill in refrigerator for 20 minutes.

4. In a large mixing bowl, beat marshmallow creme with an electric mixer until smooth. Add peanut butter and beat until smooth. Stir in whipped topping. Spoon over chocolate layer. Chill in refrigerator for at least 4 hours.

5. To serve, arrange mini pretzels around cake top and sprinkle with peanut brittle. Slice and serve chilled.

Mom's Berry Surprise

Prep 15 minutes **Bake** 29 minutes **Makes** 12 servings

- **Nonstick cooking spray for baking, *Pam*®**
- 1 **box (18.25-ounce) yellow cake mix, *Betty Crocker*®**
- 3 **eggs**
- 1 **cup buttermilk**
- ⅓ **cup vegetable oil, *Wesson*®**
- ¼ **cup water**
- 1 **teaspoon almond extract, *McCormick*®**
- 2 **cans (16 ounces each) buttercream frosting, *Betty Crocker*®**
- 2½ **cups mixed fresh berries (raspberries, blackberries, and/or blueberries), rinsed and patted dry**

1. Preheat oven to 350°F. Lightly spray two 8-inch round cake pans with baking spray; set aside.

2. In a large mixing bowl, beat cake mix, eggs, buttermilk, oil, water, and almond extract with an electric mixer on low for 30 seconds. Scrape down sides of bowl and beat on medium for 2 minutes. Transfer to the prepared pans. Bake for 29 to 34 minutes or until a tester comes away clean and cake starts to pull away from the sides of the pans. Cool in pans for 5 minutes before turning onto a wire cooling rack to cool completely.

3. Level the cakes if they have crowned and split each layer horizontally with a serrated knife. Stack the four cake layers, spreading ½ cup frosting and ½ cup berries on each of the bottom three layers before adding the next layer. Frost the outside of the cake with remaining frosting. Arrange remaining berries in a ring around the top of the cake.

Inside-Out German Chocolate Cake

Prep 15 minutes **Bake** 29 minutes **Makes** 12 servings

- **Nonstick cooking spray for baking, *Pam*®**
- 1 **box (18.25-ounce) German chocolate cake mix, *Betty Crocker*®**
- 3 **eggs**
- 1⅓ **cups low-fat chocolate milk, *Nestlé*® *Quik*®, or water**
- ½ **cup vegetable oil**
- 3 **teaspoons rum extract, *McCormick*® (optional)**
- 2 **cans (16 ounces each) coconut pecan frosting, *Betty Crocker*®**
- 1 **can (16-ounce) dark chocolate frosting, *Betty Crocker*®**

1. Preheat oven to 350°F. Lightly spray two 8-inch round cake pans with baking spray; set aside.

2. In a large mixing bowl, beat cake mix, eggs, chocolate milk, oil, and 1 teaspoon of the rum extract (if using) on low for 30 seconds. Scrape down sides of bowl and beat on medium for 2 minutes. Transfer to the prepared pans.

3. Bake for 29 to 34 minutes or until a tester comes away clean and cake starts to pull away from the sides of the pans. Cool in pans for 5 minutes before turning on to a wire cooling rack to cool completely.

4. In a medium bowl, stir together coconut pecan frosting and 1½ teaspoons of the rum extract (if using). Level the cakes if they have crowned and split each layer horizontally with a serrated knife. Stack the cake layers, spreading one-third of the coconut pecan frosting in between. Stir the remaining ½ teaspoon rum extract (if using) into the chocolate frosting and frost the outside of cake.

Citrus Marbled Pound Cake

Prep 20 minutes **Bake** 55 minutes **Makes** 8 servings

- **Nonstick cooking spray for baking, *Pam®***
- 1 **box (16-ounce) pound cake mix, *Betty Crocker®***
- ¾ **cup water**
- 2 **eggs**
- 1 **teaspoon ground ginger, *McCormick®***
- 5 **tablespoons frozen lemonade concentrate, thawed, *Minute Maid®***
- ½ **teaspoon shredded lemon zest**
- **Yellow food coloring, *McCormick®***
- 3 **tablespoons frozen orange juice concentrate, thawed, *Minute Maid®***
- ½ **teaspoon shredded orange zest**
- **Red food coloring, *McCormick®***
- 1 **cup ginger preserves, *Robertson's®***

1. Preheat oven to 350°F. Spray an 8×4-inch loaf pan with baking spray; set aside.

2. In a large mixing bowl, beat cake mix, water, eggs, and ginger with an electric mixer on low for 30 seconds. Scrape down sides of bowl and beat for 1 minute on medium. Remove half the batter to another large bowl; add 3 tablespoons of the lemonade concentrate, lemon zest, and 4 to 6 drops yellow food coloring. Beat on medium speed for 1 minute. To other half of batter, add orange juice concentrate, orange zest, 14 to 16 drops yellow food coloring, and 8 to 10 drops red food coloring. Beat on medium speed for 1 minute.

3. Alternately spoon one-third of the lemon batter and one-third of the orange batter into prepared pan, using all of the batter. Swirl with a knife to marble the batter.

4. Bake for 55 to 60 minutes or until a tester comes away clean. Remove from oven; cool completely on a wire rack.

5. For ginger glaze, in a small saucepan, melt ginger preserves and remaining 2 tablespoons of lemonade concentrate over medium heat. Remove from heat and cool to room temperature.

6. Remove cake from pan and spread ginger glaze over top. Slice and serve.

Hot Chocolate Cherry Crumble

Prep 20 minutes **Bake** 40 minutes **Makes** 8 servings

- **Nonstick cooking spray for baking, *Pam*®**
- **1 can (21-ounce) cherry pie filling, *Comstock*®**
- **1 can (15-ounce) dark sweet cherries, drained, *Oregon*®**
- **½ teaspoon almond extract, *McCormick*®**
- **1 box (6.88-ounce) chocolate biscotti, *Nonni's*®**
- **2 envelopes (1 ounce each) hot cocoa mix, *Swiss Miss*®**
- **¼ cup packed brown sugar, *C&H*®**
- **1 tablespoon all-purpose flour**
- **½ teaspoon baking powder**
- **¾ cup milk chocolate chips, *Ghirardelli*®**
- **6 tablespoons butter, melted**
- **Chocolate syrup, *Hershey's*®**

1. Preheat oven to 350°F. Spray a 9-inch square baking pan with baking spray; set aside.

2. In a large bowl, stir together cherry pie filling, cherries, and almond extract. Spoon into prepared pan; set aside.

3. In a food processor, pulse biscotti into crumbs. Add hot cocoa mix, brown sugar, flour, and baking powder; pulse until combined. In a large bowl, stir together biscotti mixture and chocolate chips. Drizzle in melted butter and stir until mixture comes together. Sprinkle over top of cherry mixture.

4. Bake for 40 to 45 minutes or until bubbling. Serve warm with a drizzle of chocolate sauce over top.

Scooter Pies

Prep 20 minutes **Bake** 15 minutes **Makes** 8 pies

- **1 sheet frozen puff pastry, thawed,** ***Pepperidge Farm®***
- **1 cup marshmallow creme,** ***Kraft®***
- **1 tablespoon butter**
- **3 tablespoons instant banana cream pudding and pie filling,** ***Jell-O®***
- **2 cups powdered sugar, sifted,** ***C&H®***
- **⅓ to ½ cup heavy cream**
- **1 teaspoon banana extract,** ***McCormick®***
- **3 to 4 drops yellow food coloring,** ***McCormick®***

1. Preheat oven to 400°F. Line a baking sheet with parchment paper and place a wire cooling rack over baking sheet; set aside.

2. On a lightly floured surface, unroll puff pastry sheet. Using a 3¼-inch round cookie cutter,* cut dough into rounds; reroll dough scraps to make eight total rounds. Place on two baking sheets, spaced 2 inches apart.

3. Bake for 15 to 18 minutes or until puffed and golden. Remove from oven and cool completely on wire racks.

4. Place marshmallow creme and butter in a microwave-safe bowl. Microwave, uncovered, on high for 1½ minutes, stirring every 30 seconds or until smooth. Stir in banana pudding mix until well mixed. Cool to room temperature.

5. In a small bowl, stir together powdered sugar, cream, banana extract, and food coloring until a smooth glaze consistency.

6. To serve, cut rounds in half horizontally. Spoon 1 heaping tablespoon of marshmallow mixture between layers. Place pies on wire cooling rack. Pour glaze over each pie. Cool completely until glaze is hard.

***Note:** If you don't have a 3¼-inch round cookie cutter, use an 8-ounce pineapple can with both ends removed.

Chocolate-Merlot Fondue

Start to Finish 15 minutes **Makes** 6 servings

DIPPING SAUCE

- 1 **cup heavy cream**
- 1 **teaspoon instant espresso powder,** ***Medaglia D'Oro®***
- 1 **package (12-ounce) milk chocolate chips,** ***Nestlé®***
- 2 **tablespoons Merlot wine**
- 2 **teaspoons vanilla extract,** ***McCormick®***

DIPPABLES

- **Frozen cheesecake balls (use a melon baller)**
- **Frozen key lime pie balls**
- **Chocolate-sour cherry bread, cut into cubes,** ***La Brea Bakery®***
- **Pound cake, cut into cubes**
- **Pumpkin bread, cut into cubes**
- **Brownies, cut into cubes**
- **Sugar cookies**
- **Shortbread**
- **Dried pineapple slices**
- **Dried mango slices**

1. For dipping sauce, in a medium saucepan, combine cream and espresso powder over medium heat. Bring to a simmer; add chocolate chips, stirring constantly until chocolate is melted. Stir in wine and vanilla.

2. Transfer sauce to a fondue pot or mini slow cooker to keep warm. Skewer your favorite dippables and enjoy!

Mocha Amour Brownies

Prep 20 minutes **Bake** 70 minutes **Makes** 16 brownies

BROWNIE LAYER

- 1 **box (19.9-ounce) fudge brownie mix, *Betty Crocker*®**
- ¼ **cup double-strength coffee, cooled, *Folgers*®**
- 2 **eggs**

TOPPING

- 1 **package (8-ounce) cream cheese, softened, *Philadelphia*®**
- 3½ **cups sifted powdered sugar**
- 2 **eggs**
- 2 **tablespoons double-strength coffee, cooled, *Folgers*®**
- 1 **can (21-ounce) cherry pie filling**

1. Preheat oven to 350°F. Line a 9×13-inch baking pan with foil. Spray with nonstick cooking spray.

2. For brownie layer, in a large bowl, stir together brownie mix, ¼ cup double-strength coffee, and 2 eggs until mixed; set aside. For topping, in a medium mixing bowl, beat cream cheese and sugar with an electric mixer until creamy. Add 2 eggs and 2 tablespoons of double-strength coffee; beat until well mixed.

3. Spread brownie batter in prepared pan. Pour cream cheese topping over brownie batter and spread to cover. Spoon cherry pie filling over the top.

4. Bake for 15 minutes. Reduce temperature to 325°F and bake for 55 minutes more. Cool in pan completely before cutting into squares.

Oatmeal-Peanut Butter Crunchies

Prep 15 minutes **Chill** 1 hour **Bake** 10 minutes per batch **Makes** 27 cookie sandwiches

COOKIES

- 1 **bag (17.5-ounce) oatmeal cookie mix, *Betty Crocker*®**
- 1 **stick (½ cup) plus 2 tablespoons butter, softened**
- 1 **egg**
- 6 **tablespoons all-purpose flour**
- ¼ **cup packed brown sugar, *C&H*®**

FILLING

- 1 **cup creamy peanut butter, *Skippy*® *Natural***
- ¾ **cup powdered sugar, sifted, *C&H*®**
- **Vanilla bean ice cream, *Häagen-Dazs*®**

1. Preheat oven to 375°F. Line baking sheet(s) with parchment paper; set aside.

2. For cookies, in a large bowl, stir together cookie mix, butter, egg, flour, and brown sugar until dough comes together. Shape dough into a 2¼-inch diameter log and wrap in plastic wrap. Chill for at least 1 hour. Slice log into ¼-inch slices. Transfer slices to baking sheets, spaced 2 inches apart. Bake for 10 to 12 minutes or until starting to brown. Remove from oven and cool on baking sheet 5 minutes. Transfer cookies to a rack to cool completely.

3. In a bowl, beat peanut butter with powdered sugar on low. Sandwich cookie bottoms together with 1 tablespoon filling. Serve with ice cream.

BananAlaska

Prep 30 minutes + final assembly **Freeze** 8 hours **Makes** 12 servings

COOKIES

- **1 roll (16.5-ounce) refrigerated sugar cookie dough, *Pillsbury*®**
- **½ cup all-purpose flour**

PUDDING

- **1 box (5.1-ounce) instant banana pudding and pie filling, *Jell-O*®**
- **3 cups cold milk**
- **1 banana, sliced**

ICE CREAM FILLING

- **1½ pints vanilla Swiss almond ice cream, softened in refrigerator for 2 hours, *Häagen-Dazs*®**
- **½ cup sliced almonds, toasted, *Diamond*®**

MERINGUE

- **1 cup pasteurized egg whites,* *Eggology*®**
- **½ cup sugar**
- **½ teaspoon almond extract, *McCormick*®**

1. Preheat oven to 350°F.

2. For cookie layers, in a bowl, knead half of the cookie dough with ¼ cup of the flour until flour is incorporated. On a lightly floured surface, roll dough to ¼-inch thickness. Using the bottom of a 9-inch springform pan as a guide, cut 1 large cookie. Repeat with remaining dough and ¼ cup of flour. Wrap both large cookies with plastic wrap; place in freezer for 15 minutes. Remove from freezer, place on cookie sheets. Bake for 15 to 18 minutes or until golden, rotating the pans halfway through cooking.

3. For pudding, in a large bowl, combine pudding mix with milk; using a wire whisk, beat for 2 minutes. Chill in refrigerator about 5 minutes or until thickened. Fold in sliced banana. Cover with plastic wrap; refrigerate until ready to assemble dessert.

4. To assemble, place one of the cookies in a 9-inch springform pan. Spread softened ice cream on cookie in pan; top with the second cookie. Spread banana pudding on cookie until smooth; sprinkle with toasted almond slices. Cover with a layer of plastic wrap and a layer of aluminum foil. Freeze for at least 8 hours, preferably overnight.

5. At serving time, preheat oven broiler to 500°F. For meringue, in a large mixing bowl, beat pasteurized egg whites with an electric mixer on medium until soft peaks form. Beat in sugar and almond extract and beat until stiff peaks form. Be careful not to overbeat. Remove dessert from freezer. Remove springform pan by first dampening a kitchen towel with hot water. Wrap towel around springform pan to loosen the dessert. Remove dessert from springform pan and place on an ovenproof platter. Cover top and sides with meringue. Place under broiler for 2 to 3 minutes or until meringue has golden peaks. Watch carefully as meringue can burn quickly. Serve immediately.

***Note:** Using pasteurized egg whites in place of fresh egg whites eliminates the risk of salmonella contamination.

Index

M

N

O

P

Q-R

your personal back stage pass to

everything Sandra Lee

Follow her on Facebook + Twitter

Join in the fun at facebook.com/SandraLee

Join Sandra on her Facebook page to interact and communicate with Sandra, her team, and other fans like you. Sandra posts frequently and you can receive recipes, videos of her cooking demonstrations, and behind-the-scene views of the making of her TV shows, "Sandra Lee's Semi-Homemade Cooking" and "Money Saving Meals" which air on Food Network. You can get in the action too—Sandra encourages you to post your comments and upload photos that show off your Semi-Homemade recipe masterpieces. Join now at facebook.com/sandralee.

Follow Sandra @sandrashm (twitter.com/sandrashm)

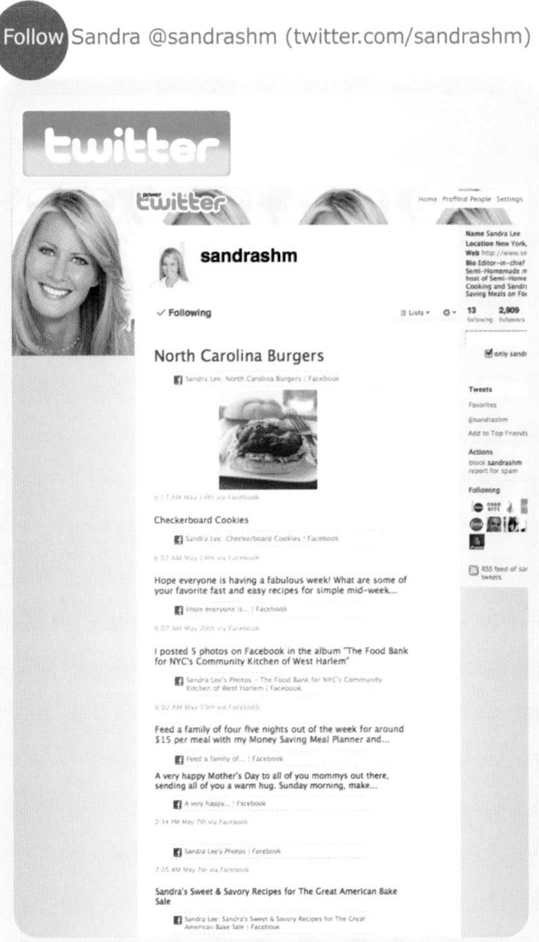

Get up-to-the-minute insights from Sandra as she tweets about her life, travels, events, the making of her TV shows, books and magazines, and more!

Be the first to know—follow Sandra now on her Twitter page!

Join Sandra's Semi-Homemakers Club today at SandraLee.com!